Naomi's Daughters

With thanks to
Amanda, Brooke, Erika, Gabrielle, Leah, Mariel,
Mélanie, and Sarah of the First United Church
Youth Group, Ottawa, who have captured the spirit of
Naomi's daughters

Naomi's Daughters

Bridging the Generations

Alyson C. Huntly

UNITED CHURCH PUBLISHING HOUSE
Toronto, Canada

Naomi's Daughters
Bridging the Generations
Copyright © 2000 United Church Publishing House

Canadian Cataloguing in Publication Data

Huntly, Alyson

    Naomi's Daughters : bridging the generations

Includes bibliographical references

ISBN 1-55134-113-1

1. United Church Women. 2. Church group work. I Title.

BX9881.H865 2000   287.9'2'082   C00-931292-7

United Church Publishing House
3250 Bloor Street West, Suite 300
Etobicoke, Ontario
Canada M8X 2Y4
416-231-5931
bookpub@uccan.org

Design, Editorial, and Production: Publishing, and Graphics and Print Units
Cover Illustration: Laura Ciruls

Printed in Canada

5 4 3 2 1   04 03 02 01 00

 990388

Contents

Part 2   Naomi's Daughters Workshops

Foreword

As a Christian feminist who reached adulthood in the 1960s, I know from experience that it is often difficult for women of different generations to understand and appreciate each other's world views and life choices. These cross-generational differences are reflected in many ways, including the manner in which women experience themselves as persons of faith and how they participate in the life of their church-community. In *Naomi's Daughters*, Alyson Huntly has created a resource that will help women, especially church women, to talk honestly and listen respectfully across the generations, and to reflect on and discuss the source and meaning of both our differences and our common ground.

Naomi's Daughters is a richly textured piece of fabric woven together by Alyson with sensitivity, integrity, and imagination. Most women connected to the United Church will recognize important strands of their experience in this book. Individual stories of United Church women, shared at workshops held across the country during 1999, make up the warp of the fabric. The woof is comprised of the shared history of women as experienced in church and society through the decades from the 1930s to the 1990s. The loom is a firmly grounded framework of relevant social/psychological theory and biblical/theological reflection. The result is a vibrant, strong, yet flexible, piece of fabric.

The Committee on Sexism, who co-sponsored the Naomi's Daughters project along with the National United Church Women, believes this resource is especially valuable at this time of review and restructuring of women's organizations and groups in the United Church. It increases understanding of the current situation as well as provides possible directions for the future. Alyson has designed the book so that it can be used in a number of ways—by individual readers, by groups that want to read and discuss the book together, or as a resource for women who are interested in re-creating the workshop experience for themselves. But no matter how and where women find themselves in the pattern, they will be enlightened, affirmed, and inspired by the weaving.

Glenys Huws
Committee on Sexism

Acknowledgements

This project has been very collaborative. The support of two organizations in the church, the General Council's Committee on Sexism and the National Consultation of the United Church Women (UCW) played a very important role in supporting, advising, funding, and critiquing. The work of the Task Group on Women in the United Church, and particularly the early research the group did into relationships across generations, also greatly informed my work. And the women in the workshops themselves, as they talked, shared experiences, and tested and prodded and challenged, shaped the contents of this book. I am responsible for what appears in the following pages, but this is by no means a solo endeavour. I am grateful for this opportunity and indebted to all who joined with me in this venture.

This project would not have been possible without the very generous financial support of the National Consultation of UCW and the Mission and Service Fund (through the Committee on Sexism of The United Church of Canada). These two groups offered their moral support and encouragement to the project, as well as making it possible to hold the development workshops in different parts of Canada.

The workshop hosts and participants were vital to the development of the content of this book. I thank them for their enthusiasm and willingness to share insights and critical feedback, as well as the gift of their time. I owe a great debt of thanks to:

Debbie Culbertson, Heather Marshall, and the women of Southminster-Steinhauer United Church, Alberta;

barb janes and the women of Selkirk United Church, Manitoba;

Peter Lougheed, Jessica McCrae, and the women of Kanata United Church, Ontario;

Susan Jackson and the women of Emmanuel-Bethany Pastoral Charge, Ontario;

Alison Nicholson and the women of Canfield Pastoral Charge, Ontario;

Kim Uyede-Kai and the women of Centennial-Japanese United Church (Toronto), Ontario;

The women of First United Church (Ottawa), Ontario;

James and Mary Webber-Cook, and the women of Tryon-Hampton Pastoral Charge, Prince Edward Island.

I am very grateful to Enid Kirkhope for her work to collect stories and preserve of the history of the UCW, and her willingness to share those stories with me.

And finally, special thanks to Jane Pearl and Karen Simonson for their invaluable research assistance and "fact finding."

Part 1

Generations of Women in the Church

Introduction

Times are changing for women in the United Church. Structures, groups, and ways of working together that have served us well for many years are not the ones that can carry us into the twenty-first century. We have known this for a while. We have sensed the tensions, felt the cracks, and wondered what was happening. When the Thirty-sixth General Council of the United Church met in Camrose in 1997, the issue of women's organizations in the church was squarely on the agenda. The Council struck a task group to determine a new structure for women's groups in the church, one better suited to the needs of women in these changing times. The Task Group on Women in the United Church consulted widely and heard from over two thousand women through-out the church about needs, structures, and issues for the variety of women's groups that now exist.

I began work on the Naomi's Daughters project around the time that the Task Group was carrying out its broad consultations. As I write this, the group is just preparing its report to the Division of Mission in Canada, in preparation to report to the Thirty-seventh General Council in 2000. The two processes are parallel in time and, to some degree, in content. Many of the issues I addressed in the workshops were similar to those the Task Group has addressed and these two pieces of work may be seen as parts of a larger entity. However, the Task Group was looking more broadly at the issues for women's groups and women's work in the church, while I was focusing on a slightly different issue—women's relationships across generations.

I set out to explore how women in the United Church relate to one another across different ages and life experiences. How are we different? What are some of the underlying issues that we struggle with as we attempt to relate across generations? What tools and strategies can help women bridge the generational divide? What are the issues that block women from coming together across barriers of age and life-experience? What are the success stories—the things that are working well? How can we build bridges of understanding and shared participation in the whole ministry of the church?

In the fall and winter of 1999, I initiated a series of workshops with women in different parts of Canada to explore these questions, as well as to develop and test some resources that might enable women to continue to reflect on these issues for themselves. The program resources, liturgy, analysis, and stories in the book have been developed out of those workshops with women of different ages, in United Church congregations in many different contexts.

They offer tools to help women throughout the church work together across the ages with greater insight, empathy, and mutual understanding.

The two parts of this book are formed out of the experiences of those workshops. The first part gives background and analysis of some of the issues affecting generations of women in the church. The content comes from the conversations in the workshops and from further reading and reflection upon what happened and what it might mean.

Interspersed throughout the first part are a series of stories of women. These stories and these characters are fictional creations. As they say in the usual disclaimers, any resemblance to individuals past or present is entirely coincidental. Although the individuals in these stories are entirely my own creation, they are real in a way. They are a creative composite—a compilation of the stories of many women throughout our church. These characters and their stories, formed in my own imagination, are another way of reflecting upon and sharing what I learned in the Naomi's Daughters workshops.

The workshop and study outlines form the second part of the book, including the activities and liturgies that I used in the workshops throughout Canada. I have arranged this material into several different formats to provide options for a variety of settings from retreats and workshops to study groups. In addition, discussion questions are provided for each chapter to allow groups or individuals to reflect on the contents of this book. All of these tools have the same general purpose—to allow groups of women of all ages to come together to reflect on what it means to be the women of the United Church into the twenty-first century.

I called this venture "Naomi's Daughters" from the outset. It was a way of naming the project, but, more importantly, I saw it as a way of naming ourselves as women in the church. For me it was a way of saying that we women in the church today are the daughters of women who have gone before us. Naomi of the biblical story doesn't have any daughters, not biological kin at any rate. But she has Ruth, a young woman who chooses to be for her a daughter worth more than seven sons, more than life itself. Ruth chooses this role freely and out of love. She does not *have* to, but she *chooses* to out of loyalty, love, and incredible faith in the future. Ruth sets her course and the whole future of her people is restored. It's not just that Ruth and Naomi hang on and manage to survive—they end up making history.

I believe this is us, as women in the church today. We are women who have chosen relationship with one another, bound together in love and commitment in this family we call church. We choose relationships with each other across the divide of generations and cultures, just as Ruth did. We choose, out of loyalty and out of love. In spite of the obstacles we face, and even with all the conflicts and tensions that have emerged in this present moment, I firmly believe this is still who we are.

We are daughters of Naomi and, in our loving relationship across the generations, we are shaping the future. In our daring and our commitment, our honesty, loyalty, trust, and challenge, we are doing far more than merely "surviving." We are not just making sure that women's organizations don't fade away or that our church doesn't die out. We are creatively living out a vision that will transform our church and our world. We *are* Naomi's daughters.

Naomi's Daughters

The Story of Ruth

> Long ago, in the days when the judges ruled, there was a terrible famine. In the land of Moab, there lived two women, and their names were Ruth and Naomi…

So begins biblical story of Ruth, a moving account of women struggling to survive in hard times. Ruth and Naomi are the central characters in this tale. Ruth, the Moabite daughter-in-law, and Naomi, her old mother-in-law. Naomi had moved to Moab to escape a terrible famine in her homeland. She moved to an alien land, and there lost her husband and both her sons to sickness and death. As the story begins, Naomi urges her widowed Moabite daughters-in-law, Orpah and Ruth, to cut their losses and return to their own families.

Naomi changes her name to Mara, "bitter," and begins the bitter journey back to her homeland. With no one to support or protect her, her life is all but over. Probably she intends to die on this futile journey home. The folk-tale style of the story leaves little doubt as to who is the heroine of the tale. Orpah, whose name means "back of the neck," turns her back on Naomi and goes home to her mother.

The biblical storyteller does not mention Orpah again, and so we are left wondering what happened to her. Did she survive? Is she really so dishonourable; after all surely she had her own mother and family to be concerned about too? But the storyteller is not really interested in those questions—Orpah is little more than a narrative device to show us what others in this situation might do, compared to the real heroine of the tale, who is Ruth.

Ruth, whose name means "companion," pledges to stay with Naomi. In one of the most oft quoted passages of all scripture, Ruth declares:

Do not press me to leave you or to turn back from following you!
Where you go, I will go;
Where you lodge, I will lodge;
your people shall be my people,
and your God my God.
Where you die, I will die—there will I be buried.
May the LORD *do thus and so to me, and more as well,*
if even death parts me from you! (Ruth 1:16–17)

And so the two women journey forward into the unknown, united by nothing but their loyalty to one another and their common need for survival; bound by no social convention or legal obligation but drawn together by the demands of their situation and their love for each other.

The plot twists and turns through the four short chapters of the story. By sheer determination, the two women eke out an existence. They gain protection in a time when there was no legal recourse for women who did not have men folk to protect them. They use their cunning and more than a little trickery to outwit their adversaries, win back Naomi's property, and gain a husband for Ruth. Through it all, Ruth's loyalty to Naomi is unwavering. The story ends with Ruth giving birth to a son, thus ensuring survival and continuity not only for herself but also for Naomi. The women of the community acknowledge that this child is indeed Naomi's heir, her future, her means of survival in old age.

> *"Blessed be the LORD, who has not left you this day without next-of-kin...He shall be to you a restorer of life and a nourisher of your old age; for your daughter-in-law who loves you, who is more to you than seven sons, has borne him." Then Naomi took the child and laid him in her bosom, and became his nurse. (Ruth 4:15–16)*

The adoption of the baby as Naomi's own symbolizes a chosen relationship, an adoption that had in fact occurred some years earlier. With the death of Naomi's son, Ruth's husband, nothing bound Ruth to Naomi. Yet, throughout the story, Ruth chose the role of an adopted daughter. She chose a relationship that the storyteller tells us was worth "more than seven sons" to Naomi. In a patriarchal culture that so valued sons, that was saying a lot! The acknowledgement of the son born to Ruth as Naomi's true heir is the storyteller's way of conveying the significance of this chosen relationship: without son or husband Naomi was sure to perish, yet because of Ruth's loyalty she did not.

In the conclusion of the story, we discover that the child born to Ruth was the father of Jesse, who was in turn the father of King David. And thus, the story of two women and their struggle for survival is transformed, in this final turn of phrase, into a story about nationhood. The history of the whole people pivots around this grand finale—the grandfather of King David, the child who was always known as "Naomi's boy."

Has it not always been so, for generations of women, that on the stories on individual lives, of birth and death and the struggle in-between, hinge the histories of nations? In this story the personal is indeed the political. In the individual day-to-day relationships are mapped the patterns of the whole fabric of the society. In the daily struggle for survival, which this story relates, the future survival of the nation is described. We thought we were going to hear a story about two women. In fact, we discover we have been told a story about the whole history of the people.

Background to the Story

The story of Ruth and Naomi is set in the time of the judges, a time long be-fore the great kings of Israel, shortly after Moses led the Exodus out of Egypt into the Promised Land. This time of the judges was the period when the land was being settled by the Israelite people. It was a time of political and social in-stability, characterized by violence and tribal in-fighting, wars with the Canaanites, and invasions by the Philistines.

The Book of Ruth has this as its setting, much the way we might say "long, long ago" to begin a tale from a bygone era. Certainly it was not written during the time of the judges. But it evokes that sense of the deep past, the way a fairy tale would for us today. The time of the judges was a time of lawlessness and chaos. Women were especially vulnerable. A strong sense of "nationhood" did not yet exist—women travelling outside their community, without the protection of their armed men folk, did so at the risk of their lives. Placing the setting "in the time of the judges" would have reminded the original audience just how great Naomi's peril was and how enormous was the risk Ruth took to leave her own home and care for her mother-in-law.

Although the story of Ruth and Naomi may have been told earlier, the story could only have been written down in its present form much later. There are certain Aramaic expressions in the book that come from a much later date, after the exile in Babylon. This is a time much later than the era of the "united Kingdom" and the reign of the great kings—David and Solomon. Thus the story must have been reedited or in some way updated as the people returned to their land after sixty years in captivity in Babylon. The biblical editors did not take such an editorial task lightly. They did so out of a deep spiritual purpose. And the purpose of this late telling of the story of Ruth has much to do with what is going on in the time after the exile. The nation is struggling to reconstruct when the people are finally permitted to return home after more than a generation of forced exile. Much has been lost—language, culture, and religious tradition. As the people return, they must reconstruct not merely the cities, farms, homes, and the Temple, but the very essence of who they are.

The land had not remained vacant during the exile—most of the nation's elite and upper classes, but not all the peasant folk, had been taken into exile. Those who remained on the land mingled and intermarried with non-Jews. As the exiles returned, some among them were determined to set apart a people defined on narrow terms by lineage and ancestry. There were strong debates about who had a claim to the land, and who didn't. There were attempts to draw lines—to define in groups and out groups, "us" and "them." Some leaders within the post-exile community were urging husbands who had married non-Jews to divorce immediately and send away wives and children, with horrific consequences for those who were sent away.

Yet there were other voices in the community, and somewhere in the mixture of opinions ran another thread, a voice for inclusion and justice. In the great storytelling tradition of the Jewish people, someone told a story, a parable for its time, about Ruth the Moabite who married outside the lines, whose remarkable courage and loyalty became a shining example of faithfulness to God, Ruth, the heroine of the story! And when the story reaches its end, lo and behold, this foreigner, this Moabite, is revealed to be the great-grandmother of the great King David, the greatest of all the kings of Israel.

The story of Ruth, retold in this context, is a parable about inclusion, about love that transcends the lines of nationhood, religion, culture, and gender. Seen in this light, Ruth may be the first great feminist epic. In a time when women and children were being discarded and sent away destitute because they could not prove their ancestry to the seventh generation, someone points out that Ruth the Moabite is worth more than seven sons! In a time some were insisting on absolute proof of pure ancestry and lineage, Ruth the foreigner is held up as an ancestor of King David.

Daughters of Naomi

There is a timeless quality to the story of Ruth. I used it in the workshops to develop this book initially because it was a story of two women whose relationship bridged generations. As we worked with the story, it took on much deeper meaning. Ruth and Naomi were not merely two women who managed to get along, a nice "mother-in-law story" to counteract negative stereotypes. These women were nation-builders. Their survival was intimately connected to the survival of the whole nation.

Naomi's daughters in the church today are the spiritual progeny of these ancient ancestors. These are the nation-builders within our churches. These are the women who, like Naomi and Ruth, helped their communities and their church weather the famines of depression or war or economic recession, or the other "famines" in women's lives—divorce, parenting, bereavement, aging, illness, poverty, violence.

The history of women in our church is a history of these "daughters of Naomi" who have built relationships, defied stereotypes, and used more than a little cunning to carve out the space that has allowed women through the ages to act and do and be the church even in times when women were not permitted access to boards or sessions or the order of ministry. To recall the story of Ruth and Naomi is to evoke the stories of women whose daily lives have built communities, built congregations, and established nations of the spirit.

When women talk about this biblical story, they recall their own much-beloved mothers-in-law and daughters-in-law who help them to survive. They remember beloved mentors, teachers, friends, companions, spiritual guides, neighbours, all those women with whom they had formed a special relationship that spanned generations. They remember women who "knew what I needed more than I knew it myself," or women who became "like a parent to me when

I came from far away," to quote women from a workshop in rural PEI.

Women in the church have a long history of loyal, caring, and creative relationships. Throughout the decades women have come together under the umbrella of church to nurture one another and their communities. From turkey suppers to luncheons at funerals, women have fed one another body and soul. Through study, spirituality, and service, they have forged bonds as strong and deep and lasting as those between Ruth and Naomi.

The story of Ruth and Naomi evokes such stories. It also calls forth a vision that is deeper and broader than any one woman's story. The story inspires us to bolder risk-taking, as it invites us, as women in the church, to step out beyond boundaries of race or age or culture or gender.

The story transcends stereotypes—those limitations we place on how women of different ages are "supposed" to relate. It redefines what family is about—not merely kinship based on blood-ties, but the deeper ties borne of faith, loyalty, love, and courage. Women can and do build relationships of care, support, trust, and friendship outside of their own generations. Older women don't always have to be the caregivers. Younger women can also be role models. Women do not have to passively accept what fate brings their way but can shape and create a new and more just future for themselves and their communities.

Discussion of passivity, roles, and expectations raised interesting questions in the workshops about the role of Orpah. The biblical storyteller may not have had much sympathy for her, but women in the workshops often did. Some saw her role as "stepping out of the traditional role of caregiver" and praised her courage and independence.

Women in one workshop spoke from their experience as second-generation Japanese Canadian women married to oldest sons. They knew that traditionally they would be expected to stay with and support their mothers-in-law without complaint. They would, they said, be obligated to care for their mothers-in-law if their husbands died. Orpah left Naomi and disappeared from the story. Yet, in many ways, the women of Japanese ancestry saw her action as far more radical than that of Ruth. Orpah did something many Asian women would like to have done, but didn't feel they had any choice about. Within the biblical context, Ruth's actions were the daring and unexpected ones. In the Asian context, Orpah was the one who broke new ground.

From either perspective, however, the story clearly pointed women towards a conversation about stepping out of conventional roles, duties, and expectations. The audacity with which Naomi and Ruth fight for their right to survive reminds me of the outrageousness of Nellie McClung, who noted that "the women may lift mortgages or build churches or any other light work, but the real heavy work of the church, such as moving resolutions in the general assemblies must be done by strong, hardy men!" (McClung 1972,

72). The persistence with which these two women insist on surviving reminds me of how women in the church have bonded together to survive. I think of those examples of women who, when excluded from the boardrooms or meetings of elders, quietly occupied the kitchen. Or, when denied the right to be "ministers," set up their own mission boards, raised their own funds, and simply set about doing ministry in the world.

The story also moves us to a spiritual plane. Ruth's model of faithful love is a parable not just about human relationship but also about God. "This is what God is like," said a workshop participant. This is indeed God's voice, in story form, calling us to deeper connection with one another. This is God's voice, beckoning us into relationships that cross the boundaries and reshape the borders—in our own lives and in our communities. This is God's voice calling us to dare new paths, to transcend what we know, and to leave behind the old.

Visions for Women in the Church

In the workshops, I used the story of Ruth and Naomi as a starting point for asking women about their vision for how women in the church could relate across generations. What are the elements of this vision?

- many cultures and many generations working together
- welcome and acceptance of all
- inclusion
- breaking down isolation
- mutual respect and understanding
- joy
- shared leadership
- outreach
- nurture
- breaking down barriers
- crossing boundaries

All the elements they named can be found within the story of Ruth and Naomi.

I continue to be amazed by the clarity of the vision that was expressed in the Naomi's Daughters workshops and by how many commonalities I found in very different contexts. Many items appeared in almost every expression of vision, for example, inclusiveness and shared food! Women from rural PEI to small-town Manitoba, urban Alberta, or inner-city Ottawa expressed a deep longing to connect across generations, to hear one another's stories, to be together, and to learn from one another.

The depth of this longing surprised me—the idea for this book came out of a struggle that might have been characterized as a generation gap or even a generation conflict. It was very clear, at least in the groups with which I gathered, that women have a hope and vision for something that would bring them together across the barriers or differences that divide them. They have memory and experience of cross-generational relationships that worked.

They know what it's like and they want more. They want to be there for one another, and they want other women to be there for them. They want to respect and be respected, and they long to understand one another better.

There is no question that this is a crisis point for women in the church; this is a turning point in terms of the structures and institutions that have been the cornerstone of women's work for nearly sixty years. Perhaps that is why the story of Ruth and Naomi strikes such a chord. It is, after all, a story of rebuilding from the bottom up. Two women, who have lost all that they hold dear, start over. A nation, struck down and all but destroyed, begins to rebuild from the ground up.

There is no question that there is deep pain, a great sense of loss, and conflict, even perhaps a sense of betrayal within the church today. Women in the United Church often feel they don't understand, or aren't understood by, women older or younger than themselves. They find it hard to connect at times because it feels as though their experiences and needs are so different. They sometimes express a feeling that they are still searching for community with one another and the search is hard.

But push the question to a deeper level and one seems to uncover a core value. Naomi's daughters know who they are and where they have come from. They know that long ago, in a time when judges ruled, there were two women whose relationship created a nation. They know that there was a time when women came together across generations, to form relationships that transformed the world. They remember the work, the community, the commitment, and the inspiration of women throughout the ages.

Dreaming of a Common Language

I have a confession to make. I have never been a member of the United Church Women. I have attended meetings occasionally, as an invited guest. I have eaten at numerous teas, sampling the cakes and work-of-art sandwiches with admiration and appreciation. I have even had the honour of sitting at the head of the table, to pour from a ceremonial teapot. But I have never been an "insider" who helped plan such an event. I have never been a member, never said "we" in reference to the UCW. I am a United Church woman, of course, but it is of the lower case variety.

In the mid-eighties I moved to a new city and joined a new congregation. In the spring of that first year, I received a letter from the UCW inviting me to participate in a phantom tea. The real tea had ceased to exist. The group, women now mostly in their seventies, simply no longer had the energy to pull it off. This virtual tea was a pen and paper invitation to contribute money in lieu of cakes and sandwiches that women might otherwise donate. It had been devised to replace the actual tea of years gone by.

Another confession. I never gave money to the phantom tea. I read the letter that year and every subsequent year with a mixture of puzzlement and guilt. But when I donated money I gave directly to the congregation. I did so through my envelopes on a regular basis, and as generously as I could, but I never gave money directly to the UCW. I probably would have declined the offer to bring a pie, had it come to that.

The UCW never felt like something that included me. It was not of my generation. Somehow, I, at the tail end of the baby-boomers, belonged to another time. The UCW, it seemed to me then, was of another era—the era of my mother and grandmothers. Between them and me there was a chasm, a vast and mysterious void. It is this sense of distance that I set out to explore in the Naomi's Daughters workshops.

Generations

This chasm between the generations did not exist in the same way for previous generations of women—the generations of my mother, grandmothers, and great-grandmothers. They joined in a continuous lineage into the groups of women in the church that preceded them. Then, at some point in time, a line was drawn. It is hard to pinpoint exactly when this happened, and perhaps it was at different times in different communities. However, gradually, in most places, women of "my generation" started to move separately from "their generation," into other kinds of women's groups, into other places within the church. I, and many others like me, did not find ourselves at home within the UCW.

I have tremendous respect for the UCW and for the wonderful work it has accomplished. I know that nowhere else in the church has there been such dedication and commitment, such deep faith and faithful service. I have long known that if you want something done, and done well, in the United Church, you can count on the UCW to do it. They have been our financial backbone, our conscience in the concerns of the world, our mission and outreach workers, our social change agents, our eyes and ears open to study and reflection, our community of pastoral care. All this I have received as a legacy and an inheritance. All of this I value and respect.

I recently attended a worship service commemorating the UCW women of my home congregation. This UCW group was the last of a long line of different units that had met over the years. At one time there would have been three or four units meeting at the same time. This last group, having stretched tenuously into the twenty-first century, was finally disbanding. I was moved to tears by the testimony to the work and service they had contributed over many long years. I felt a great stirring of pride at what these women have been and done. I stood with others for the longest standing ovation I have ever experienced in a church.

The UCW has provided its members quality of community. I admire, even envy, the way it connected so many parts of women's lives—social, family, spiritual, work, service, community. My life seems so fragmented in comparison. Different institutions and organizations meet different needs. It isn't all housed or centred on the church. There are times when I yearn for the sense of community and continuity across generations. I look back longingly on that time when lives and relationships were woven together into an integrated whole, across age groups, across the various facets of daily life. I live many miles away from my parents, and have lived most of my life a continent away from my grandmother and other older relatives. That is a loss for people of my generation.

Many women in the UCW who look out from the other side of the chasm are sad. I sense their grief and loss, as they watch a treasured organization slowly age and sometimes disband. I know that they look to me and women of my age, sometimes with resentment and certainly with questions.

- Why didn't we join?
- How is it that we managed to convey such a sense of devaluation for all that they had done?
- Why have we never evolved a mutual understanding?
- What is it that separates the generations of women in our church?
- What is the nature of this chasm that seems to divide one generation from another?

Are There Bridges That We Can Build?

That is where this book project began for me as I sat, looking out across the gap of generations and wondering.

I began this project by rereading the biblical story of Ruth and Naomi. That was my starting point for thinking about women relating to each other across generations, and also where I started the workshops. We see in this story two generations of women who shared a deep bond, forged out of mutual respect and deep trust. The story makes us wonder at the times our current generations of women have misunderstood one another. The story seems to evoke a deep longing in us, as women of the United Church.

The Workshops

These longings and hopes came through loud and clear in the Naomi's Daughters workshops. Women of all ages long to hear one another's stories, long to really know one another across this apparent generation gap. Said one participant, "I would hope that women in the church would feel comfortable enough to share their feelings with each other, whatever their ages."

The storytelling in the workshops seemed to whet women's appetites for more. "We need to have conversation across the generations, to hear one another's stories," is how one woman expressed it. Younger women talked about "mining the wisdom of older women" and sharing skills. There was a sense of urgency about not wanting to lose out on this valuable resource. Women of all ages genuinely wanted to be able to learn from each other, and younger women often looked to older ones as mentors.

"Their experiences of life are so different; we don't want to lose this!" said one young woman in her twenties. "I love the contact with women of my grandmother's generation because their lives have been so different from mine—particularly in a spiritual sense."

We see in this biblical story of Ruth and Naomi a relationship of strength and mutual support that makes us long to experience support and care from one another, in the ways that our grandmothers and great-grandmothers and great-great-grandmothers seem to have supported and cared for other generations. Women are looking for support and breaking down of the sense of isolation that they so often feel. They are looking to other women who can be there in times of need, who can give encouragement, even simply a friendly phone call to say hello.

"We should be able to depend on each other for help and support and know that other women can relate to our situation," said one woman, "especially because we are not always near the women in our own family, as it was when I grew up." It is true that many women are far from their families, and from the traditional intergenerational relationships of daughter-mother-grandmother. Single women are raising families alone; older women are experiencing an increasing sense of isolation as they age.

Women also are seeking ways to connect with women of other generations simply for the joy of it. "We should take advantage of every opportunity to be together," they said, recalling the teas and the picnics and the memorable moments over the years—from kitchen sinks to sick beds to quilting. Women of all ages have fun with each other when they get together. They may bring different gifts, but if the laughter and enthusiasm in the workshops is any indicator, women of all ages do have a good time when they meet! One women thought that perhaps, "the younger women bring enthusiasm and energy and enjoyment to learn, while the older women bring their wisdom and calmness and help others find a centre point in their lives."

Above all, it seemed to me, women were looking for a sense of mutual understanding, a common language with which to talk and share and be together. Women are looking for opportunities to share their experiences and build more of a sense of connection between older and younger. "There needs to be a thread of understanding that connects generations," is how one older women expressed it. Women have often felt devalued by each other, it seems, and spoke of wanting to hear one another more fully, and to genuinely value and respect differences.

And finally, just as Naomi and Ruth worked together to survive, women of different generations in the church also genuinely want to work together to help all women survive. Women in the workshops articulated a vision of working "on issues affecting all of us as women" such as child care, elder abuse, or violence. They talked of working together as partners in mission in the world. They envisioned women of all ages working together to make our church a place of hope, love, and compassion. They talked of ways they might work together in the wider mission of the church in the world.

Some History

Some women are longing for what we have never experienced. Some women are mourning what *was*. The UCW, and its predecessors the Woman's Missionary Society and Woman's Association, represented a strong and vital network of women that spanned age groups and met a variety of needs in the church, in the world, and for the women who participated.

"When I came to this church, ten years ago, there were three UCW circles. I don't think there are any active now. This is partly because of how busy women are today," said one woman. Her words are tinged with regret. It's not just the busyness that women remarked on, but also the fragmentation. If women's groups do still exist in congregations, often they are divided by function and age. A typical pattern is: younger women meet to discuss or reflect on their spirituality and don't want the demands of bake sales or fundraising; older women meet as the UCW and try very hard to keep holding it all together.

Clearly this is a major turning point for the church. The UCW continues to be a vital and important organization. Many women find their spiritual and community home there. It gives an outlet for their creativity, their commitment, their sense of mission, and their spiritual expression. However, there are signs that many UCW groups are struggling to maintain themselves. The organizational structures of the UCW—presbyterial, conference, and national levels—also have had a difficult time. There just aren't as many women willing to take leadership, and women who have been in leadership roles are often tired and burnt out, or overloaded with many responsibilities at many different levels of the structure.

The overall numbers tell a tale as well. In the early 1960s, membership in the UCW represented nearly 40% of the total membership of the United Church. In other words, if half the members were women, then about 80% of women were part of the women's organizations. By 1998, only 14% of United Church women were part of a women's organization, and that percentage included a whole variety of women's organizations including the UCW. The UCW was a fraction of its former size.

The women's organizations have been vital to the financing of our church. In the 1940s and 1950s, over 40% of the church's budget was raised by the women. In the mid-1960s, women's organizations accounted for over 20% of the church's fundraising efforts. By the 1990s, that figure had dropped to a smaller, but still very significant 15%. Numbers tell another tale—for the most part younger women are not joining the UCW. Part of the decline reflects an aging organization that is not replenishing its numbers.

There have been signs of problems for some time now. The 1996 *Year Book* of the United Church contained a telling comment. Hidden within the charts and statistics were these words from the statistical report:

> Membership in women's organizations, primarily the United Church Women, dropped 2.2% in 1995…As stated in last year's report, the UCW's membership is aging and fewer younger women are able or willing to belong to women's organizations. This foretells of future declines in UCW membership, declines that will have an impact on the church in several key areas: contributions to the Mission and Service Fund, contributions to congregations for local support, and in the use of mission education study and programme resources. (128)

The 1997 General Council of the United Church created a Task Group on Women in the United Church. The task group was given responsibility for discerning how women's groups in the church might best be structured, in light of what was happening throughout the church. The task group began with a survey to find out from women themselves what they saw taking place within women's organizations in the church. The survey found that, not surprisingly, most local UCW groups were very involved in fundraising and that, often, their local congregation was vitally dependent on the revenue they raised. However, the women in these groups frequently felt the burden of this dependency. Although they were proud of their contribution, they were also tired. Few women found the endless hard work to be a source of great satisfaction.

Every respondent commented on the wonderful personal support that they found within women's organizations—the friendships, encouragement, help in times of crisis, and spiritual nurture. The UCW responses indicated a tremendous loyalty to this organization. Most UCW groups expressed a wish that younger women would join them to keep their organization alive. Many indicated, with great sadness, that they had little hope for the future of their organization because this was not happening.

One older woman in one of the Naomi's Daughter's workshops commented with regret that "the older women have done their time, and now it's time for the younger women to take over and keep things going." I thought of the story of Ruth and Naomi, and of the much vilified sister-in-law, "back of the neck" Orpah, who turned her back to Naomi. Perhaps these women who have been so loyal to their own organization are wondering where are the Ruths of today.

I don't think that this is merely an issue of the loss of any one particular organization, however. The UCW is not very old, even by United Church standards. It came into being only in 1962, as a merger of two existing women's organizations—the Woman's Association and the Woman's Missionary Society. Both those organizations had a long history of involvement, in fundraising and community building within congregations, and study and outreach into the wider community and the world.

I wonder if it is not the UCW per se that women are mourning, but what it stands for—women working together across age groups, in mission, spirituality, study, service, and support. Within the UCW, women found a way to be involved in making decisions and controlling their own finances and organizational structure—sources of power and involvement that were blocked to them in the earlier days of a more male-led church. Within the UCW, women found community, support, nourishment of their minds and spirits, and opportunities to live out their faith.

These are the very things that women in the Naomi's Daughters workshops said they wanted and needed—community, involvement, spirituality, nurture, faith expression, and cross-generational encounters. And they expressed a clear willingness and interest in meeting at least some of these needs with women of different age groups from themselves. And yet something has happened to create a sense of difference and division between women of different age groups. For, as much as women might express an interest in coming together, there are differences that seem to drive them apart. Women long for common language with which to share their common vision: What is keeping them apart?

3

Generations of Women

As I write this, I have two candles burning beside me on the desk. They are the same candles that I used in the Naomi's Daughters workshops out of which this book evolved. At each workshop I asked the oldest and youngest women in the group to each light a candle. Thus two candles burned at every event, a reminder of the span of ages in the room.

They burn now as I write, reminding me of 150 women from different parts of Canada who gathered to talk about generations of women in the church. The candles have become an important symbol of the 150 life experiences of women ranging in age from the youngest—in their mid-teens—to the oldest—in their late eighties. I am somewhere in the middle of this span of nearly seventy-five years. I am young by the standards of the oldest, and yet already somewhat old from the perspective of the youngest. I feel as though I am in the middle, aware of how very different my world and my world view is from both ends of this spectrum.

Change
The world in which I grew up was light years different from the world of those women in their eighties who met with me in the Naomi's Daughters workshops. Change has always been a part of my world, and very rapid change at that. When I read Alvin Toffler's book *Future Shock*, in the early 1970s, I wasn't particularly shocked, not even very surprised. I didn't fear change in those days. Even after reading Toffler I did not find myself very concerned. After all, rapid change was as natural to me as the air I breathed. I didn't expect things to stay the same or "go back to the way they were" because "the way things are" was an ever-changing scene. All my life I have lived in a world in which change is taken for granted. As I have worked on this project, I have realized that this and other facets of my experience shaped my consciousness and the consciousness of my generation. It shaped our way of looking at the world in such a fundamental way that our whole outlook was different from those generations for whom change was an unwelcome aberration. It was almost as though we inhabited different planets, we saw things so differently.

And yet my world view is different again from those at the youngest end of this age-continuum. When my teenage daughter says to me, "Mum, you just don't understand," there is a way in which she is absolutely right. I don't, because the world in which she is growing up and becoming an adult is so vastly changed from the one in which I did my growing up—orders of magnitude different. There has been, by any measure, more change in the years between her and me than between me and my grandmother or even my great-grandmother.

I have come to believe that we, as women of the church, look out on the world and upon the church through different lenses—perspectives that are shaped by what is going on in the formative years of our adolescence and early adulthood. These lenses shape how we understand reality, and how we understand, or fail to understand, one another. Until we understand these lenses, or "frameworks" as some have called them, we will never be able to understand one another. Until we can fully name and appreciate our differences, we will not be able to claim and celebrate our commonalities.

As I write this, I often use the first person, speaking out of my late-baby-boomer framework. I have done this intentionally, not in order to remain fixed in that perspective but to openly name and acknowledge that this is where I come from. This is my starting point. In order to understand the framework of others, we must begin with an understanding of ourselves.

It is very hard to see one's own culture of course. It's like that experience we Canadians have with our own brand of English. We don't notice our own "accent" because it sounds unaccented, "normal." We don't notice that we punctuate our sentences with "eh" until we encounter those who use "huh." Similarly with culture, our own cultural framework seems to be such a given that we don't even know it is there, until we try to communicate with those of other cultures and find ourselves colliding with different perspectives, like walls of glass we don't even know are there. And so I have tried to be conscious of my own "accent" as I write, in order to be aware that I bring my own generational framework to this writing task.

Generational Differences

Generations have their own cultures, their own framework. Often in the church our frameworks have collided without us even knowing what has hit us. In order to understand one another better, in order to bridge the generations, we have to find out more about these generational differences. What happened to create this vast gap in generations?

In 1970, Margaret Mead published a remarkable little book called *Culture and Commitment* in which she outlines what underlies the present generation gap. In previous generations, children and youth learned primarily from their forebears, says Mead. Culture and knowledge were passed on with such unchanging continuity that knowledge would have seemed almost to be inherited. Change was so slow that it was barely perceptible. The old were needed to guide the young; the young learned all they needed to know from the old.

As Mead points out, the basic questions of identity—who I am; what is the nature of my life; how I speak, eat, make a living, become a parent, worship, and celebrate are all essentially predetermined within a traditional society. It is possible to fail at any of these cultural expectations, but the boundaries and rules are firmly established. Everyone learns the same answers to the basic questions of culture and survival. In such societies, the oldest members (parents and a very few grandparents or great-grandparents who survived into old age) knew what it was like to be young, because they had been young once themselves. And they knew what the young needed to learn in order to survive and become old themselves.

In certain circumstances this traditional mode of passing on culture breaks down. Events such as environmental catastrophe, emigration, or the introduction of new technology create situations in which the older generation, once essential to the passing on of knowledge and culture, become in some way redundant or out of step with the changes that have taken place. The old are no longer the experts; they no longer know any more than anyone else how to survive in the new environment. The younger generation is forced to learn and adapt primarily with its own resources. Mead sees this kind of situation as a transition to our present era in which the young, rather than learning from their elders, are in fact teaching the old how to adapt to the rapidly changing world of the technology-driven twenty-first century.

As Mead explains,

> Today, everyone born and bred before World War II is such an immigrant in time—as her forebears were in space—struggling to grapple with the unfamiliar conditions of life in a new era. Like all immigrants, in time or space, this older generation is the bearer of an old culture. (Mead 1970, 72)

Mead likens the younger generation, today's youth in Canada for example, to a first generation born into a new country. They are, much like children of immigrants, the first generation to grow up in this "new land."

Children of non–English speaking immigrants often teach the older generation the new culture. I think of those occasions in doctors' offices, banks, schools, or post offices when I have seen children of immigrants showing their elders the ropes or translating for them. They don't just translate the words of the new language. They also translate the culture—this is how things are done here, they explain.

I recall one particularly striking example in our neighbourhood. On the first day of school, I watched a kindergarten-aged child and his non–English speaking grandfather. The older man simply did not know what to do and, of course, neither did the child. But it was the child who figured it out first; by talking to his peers he learned where they were supposed to go and what they were supposed to do. Then, he took his grandfather by the hand and led him to the kindergarten door to join the group of other parents. When the time came, the child hugged his grandfather goodbye and marched confidently in the door with the other children.

In the same sort of way, says Mead, the youth of today teach older generations how to cope and survive in the "new land" of the present times. It is as standing joke in many household that if adults want to solve a computer problem, or program their VCRs, or deal with any of a host of other complex technological problems, they ask the teenagers! And I have to confess that my seven-year-old is rapidly becoming a source of technological information for me. But this is just a symptom of a much deeper change in social relationships and of the vast changes with which older generations must cope.

Change in our modern society continues to be so rapid that many of us find ourselves struggling hard to keep up. I do ask my teenage son, or even my seven-year-old, to teach me certain things because it's a shortcut in a world in which there is so much for me to learn. They are growing up in a new era so changed from the past that already it is starting to feel like a foreign land to me. And I am only in my early forties! It would be simple if the changes were only technological ones. They are not, of course. But technology has been the driver, and it has had an impact on how and where we work; how we spend our non-working hours; how we interact and communicate; how or whether we meet our basic needs for food, housing, and clothing; and a whole host of other things. When my seven-year-old talks about "those big black CDs that they used to have in the olden days," I laugh, reminding myself that if I told her she "sounded like a broken record" she wouldn't have a clue what I was talking about. There are many times when we talk across a gap of generation, as women in the church, without really understanding what the other is talking about.

The implications of this generation gap are immense. As Mead points out, "Even very recently, our elders could say, 'I have been young and you have never been old.' But today's young people can reply: 'You have never been young in the world I am young in, and you never can be'" (Mead 1970, 63). And so, my teenage daughter is right when she says I do not understand her or her world. How could I possibly? The scope of change, of course, is far deeper than simply who learns from whom. The whole structure of authority is challenged and reorganized when youth no longer look to their elders as a source of knowledge and authority for how to live and survive in the world.

Mead uses adjectives like "lonely" and "isolated" to describe today's generations. At times generations do indeed seem separated from each other by a vast gap of understanding, each unable to experience what the other has experienced. We are lost, says Mead, until we can fully grasp this and can acknowledge the gap that exists. As long as older generations continue to think we can know what it's like to be young simply by recalling what that was like for us, this gap in understanding cannot be bridged.

I know that I have reacted this way sometimes with my eldest daughter, tending to want to gloss over the differences between us. I want to claim that I do understand what her world is like, because I was young once myself. I felt that reaction at times during the Naomi's Daughters workshops as well. When younger women point out the differences in perception or world view to people of my age, I and others seemed to want to defend ourselves and claim that we really do understand—that we're all the same underneath. When women of my age touched on the differences between ourselves and women who are thirty or forty years older, I noticed a similar reaction from the older women. At some level all of us do know the differences are there, but we want to deny that reality. We cannot, however, ignore the extent to which the world has changed.

Nowhere was I more struck by how fast change has happened in our society than when meeting with women in rural PEI. As women told their stories, I listened with amazement. It is hard to fathom the scope and scale of such changes or how sweeping the impact has been. Many in the group recalled the days "before the Trans-Canada" when people could not leave their farmhouses during spring thaw because the rough, red dirt roads were impassable for horse or cart or human. You literally holed up. Women made sure their households were well stocked with winter provisions and waited for the roads to dry. It really wasn't such a long time ago, they said.

Within the living memory of many who gathered in that circle, an 8-kilometre (5-mile) trip to the next community was a major journey, and, at certain times of the year, completely out of the question. Now there is a fixed link, year-round highway to the mainland; on virtually any day of the year they could make a day-run shopping trip to the next province!

The women recalled another big change—the day that television arrived on the island. One remembered a neighbour inviting them in for the inaugural turning on of the television set his son had sent him from Montreal. The neighbours and friends gathered around. The knob was turned, as everyone waited with bated breath. There was nothing on the screen but snow. Endless patient tinkering failed to produce a TV image that day. In fact, it was two years before it would—the transmission tower in Charlottetown had not yet been constructed. But after TV came a plethora of other electronic media. This group had witnessed the passing from a time when there was no rural electricity or phones, to an era of world wide telecommunication via the Internet.

A young woman recalled a great-grandmother who never left the island. She noted, with sadness, that she will almost certainly move away for work. Most young people do; there aren't that many jobs here. Transience and urbanization have gone hand in hand with technological change. According to data gathered by Reginald Bibby, in 1945, 36 percent of Canadians had never travelled outside their home province. By 1994, in comparison, 64 percent of Canadians had travelled outside their province. Well over half of all Canadians went outside the country in that one year alone (1995, 17). We have gone from being a predominantly rural society to a predominantly urban one in less than a lifetime. The time, not long ago, when most people in Canada born, grew up, lived, worked, raised families, and died in the same community are long gone.

The oldest members of the group that gathered in PEI grew up in integrated communities. Not only did people know each other, the very fabric of their lives was woven together. They lived alongside each other, worked with each other, bought and sold from one another, attended one another's rites of passage, and socialized together. During the teen years of the oldest members of this group of women, church was the centre of community and social life. The church was the place where generations of women worshipped, baked pies, stitched quilts, held their infant sons and daughters for baptism, talked about their lives, or hosted church suppers. Church was where you gathered, celebrated, mourned, marked the passages of life, met people, or simply passed time. The little churches at the centre of each community stand now like markers of a bygone era. Transportation technology shrank the distances between them. There is no longer a "need" for a church every 8 kilometres (5 miles) and, with fewer people attending church regularly, amalgamations have been inevitable. As urbanization continues, and rural areas in Canada become more and more depopulated, there are more amalgamations, more little churches forced to close.

Technological change has brought with it compartmentalization and specialization. People no longer work with the people in their neighbourhood. Even in smaller or more remote communities, it is rare if not impossible to find the same kind of integration of work, social life, spirituality, and family that older generations took for granted.

The nature of work has changed. Consideration of issues like "unemployment rates" and "job security" is a recent phenomenon for women who grew up in an era when a career was something you did for your whole life. Canadians who work are working longer hours. More Canadians are self-employed or under-employed. Telecommuters, who do their work from home-based offices, communicating with their own or other businesses via the electronic media of phone, fax, or computer, are a more recent development.

Differences from how we raise our children to our economic circumstances to our hopes for the future or the constantly changing roles of women and the family leave many unsettled in their relationships with other generations. "We are growing up in different generations," said one woman who participated in a Naomi's Daughters workshop. "We are finding we are not able to understand each other because we haven't lived through certain circumstances. Sometimes it feels as though we just can't relate!"

Martha's Circle

Peggy Foster set up mugs on a tray for her friends in Martha's Circle. She deliberately used the regular everyday mugs. Last time Spirit of Sophia met they'd used the Centennial tea service and they had chipped a gold rim on one of the cups. While Betty and Mary cleared the remains of the pie dough from the counter, Mavis wrapped the last of the pies. "That's four hundred peach pies ready to go," announced Mavis proudly. "Martha's Circle has done it again!"

Peggy was just about to make the tea when Janet O'Neill came into the kitchen, with three-year-old Meagan in tow. "Hello ladies," she called out. "Just coming to check on the juice supply for Sunday." Janet paused to admire the pies. "Wow, will you look at this! You must be so proud. I wouldn't know what to do with a pie crust if it hit me in the face!" Meagan, who had a very good idea what one did with a pie crust, began poking the edge of one of the pies.

"No Meagan, don't touch," said Janet, as Mrs. Turner hastily moved the pie out of reach. "Well, gotta' run. Blaise has his first soccer game this afternoon, and I'm supposed to be helping with snacks. See you tomorrow!"

Peggy Foster sighed. She liked Janet, and she knew she was having a hard time, but she couldn't help being annoyed by her all the same. Meagan seemed out of hand, and Blaise was one of these children they called "attention deficit."

"In our day, they called it 'bad behaviour' and parents did something about it," she'd said stiffly once to Mrs. Newberry. Mrs. Newberry had nodded. The kids were a handful, to be sure, but Janet always seemed so unstructured somehow, as though she didn't quite know what to do.

Peggy suggested they have their tea in the parlour. "Time we put our feet up," agreed Thelma Norris cheerfully. At eighty-nine, Thelma was the oldest member of the group, but still a going concern. Thelma used to be a member of the old UCW Challenge Unit, but when that group stopped meeting so often she'd joined up with Martha's Circle. The Challenge Unit did meet when the weather was good, and of course they still helped with the spring tea, but the group wasn't nearly so active as it used to be.

The women were just clearing away the last of the tea things when Jodi Morrison came into the kitchen. "Camille said it would be okay if I picked up my pie order early," she announced. "The Spirit of Sophia group is meeting at my place tonight and I thought some of your wonderful peach pie would be a real treat."

Someone else who wouldn't know what to do with a pie crust if it hit her in the face, Mavis thought to herself. A whole group of them, in fact! How could a woman reach the ripe old age of forty-five and not know how to bake a decent peach pie? But at least they wouldn't be chipping the Centennial china.

Mavis had once suggested that Spirit of Sophia come and help with the annual pie baking. She'd even wondered if they would like to learn how to make a nice peach pie for themselves. Now hadn't that idea taken off like a lead balloon. Too busy, they'd said, making it clear they were definitely not interested in doing much work around here, but they had offered to make a donation "in lieu of pies."

"At least they're meeting and there's a group of them," she thought, trying to be generous. But somehow every time Sophia's Circle met, something happened that irritated her. It wasn't just the chipped cup, it was other things as well. That huge purple banner of ladies dancing that appeared in the sanctuary right where the memorial flag was supposed to be. Or the time Spirit of Sophia led the Lord's Prayer and changed the words to Mother-Father-God.

Peggy didn't so much mind the Lord's Prayer, though she too hated the purple ladies. Mostly, Peggy resented the fact that the Sophia women seemed to have lots of time to meet for their spirituality thing but no time to help bake pies or take a shift on kitchen duty. It was hard not to be resentful of a group that only seemed interested in doing what *they* wanted to do, and not picking up any of the load the rest of them were carrying.

Peggy hated the pie baking. She looked at her wrinkled, peach-stained hands. Her feet ached. She would be glad to get home and put her feet up. Sometimes she wondered what would happen when the women in Martha's Circle got as old as the Challenge Unit. "We're not as young as we used to be. We won't be able to carry on with this forever, but then what?" she worried. Spirit of Sophia sure didn't seem likely to pick up the torch when they were ready to pass it on.

On the way out the door, Peggy picked up the pile of *Mandates* for the study session next Thursday. Maybe they should invite Spirit of Sophia to hear the mission speaker with them. No, not on a weekday morning; Spirit of Sophia didn't do weekdays. Perhaps the women who worked out of their home like Lucy, or Stephanie, who only worked part-time? She rejected that idea before she even reached the door.

Spirit of Sophia

Jodi Morrison put out the cups and forks, still debating with herself about paper plates. In the end she decided on china. She'd save the dishes for tomorrow morning.

"At least if someone chips one of these I won't be in the dog house for life," she thought as she arranged the coffee mugs. She set out the candle that the group used at all its gatherings. It was a circle of women gathered around a well in the centre. She lit the candle as the doorbell rang. It was Clare Douglas. Clare greeted Jodi with a big hug. "How's it going with Rebekah," she asked, but Jodi didn't have time to reply before Anna and Joanna came in.

They kicked their shoes onto the mat. "What a week!" moaned Joanna. I had Nicky home from school two days and now Sam has the same bug! And I've got that major presentation for the finance department on Monday!"

"Boy am I glad those days are done," said Jodi. "Now the only kid crisis I have are the ones I can't do anything about!" Jodi's girls were both in high school this year, but Rebekah, Jodi's youngest, was almost failing. Jodi had told the group at the last meeting that she strongly suspected a drug problem.

"Hey, pie! Did you get this from the church?" Anne pulled up a chair at the table.

"That was brave of you, Jodi," remarked Clare. "Lucky you didn't have to stay and make them. Did they mention the teacup?"

"No, I'd already offered to try to replace it but they said you can't get that pattern anymore. They'll probably just lock up all the cupboards again."

"Hi. Sorry I'm late," Lucy hung her coat on the back of a chair. "By the way, we got another letter about kitchen patrol." There was a collective moan from the group.

"I don't see why we can't just add a couple of hours to Ed's time. I'd rather pay him to clean the kitchen when he does the rest of the basement."

"They don't like that idea, I think they think it's a huge luxury to even have a caretaker" said Lucy. "They want each women's group to take a turn once a month."

"It makes me feel like Mum is telling me to clean up my room," said Clare.

"They won't like the way we clean it either," Jodi added. "And what if we chip another golden goblet? They'll probably lock us out of the entire building!"

"There's no way I can give up a Saturday morning a month to clean another kitchen," said Clare. "I barely get my own kitchen cleaned!"

"I *don't* get mine done. I'm giving up cleaning for Lent!" laughed Joanna, "Or at least until flu season is over."

"I think we're just going to have to be clear on this one," said Anne. "They don't want us to use the kitchen and we don't want to clean it. Let's just say we'll never use the kitchen again. Period."

"Is Janet O'Neill coming tonight?" Lucy figured it was better to change the subject.

"I don't think so," Jodi replied. "She doesn't like to get a babysitter on the weekends the kids are with her."

"Those are the times she probably most needs a break," remarked Lucy.

"To tell you the truth, I'm a bit worried about her," said Anne thoughtfully. "She seems so overwhelmed at the moment."

"It's always like that, when you first separate," said Clare, who had reason to know.

"Yeah, but I mean *really* overwhelmed," Anne replied.

"Not like the rest of us who are just average, everyday overwhelmed," quipped Jodi, but she made a mental note to give Janet a call.

The Youth Group

They were meeting during the last half of the service, their usual time slot, but the girls preferred to call it Youth Group, rather than Sunday school. There were no boys, not because they weren't welcome. Just that none came.

Sylvie told everyone, in graphic detail, about the guide to better sex she found in her parents' bedroom. There were disgusted groans from everyone except Angie Henders, who was trying to think how to get the conversation back to the lesson. Sometimes it really was hard to tell what was the lesson and what wasn't. The youth leaders' handbook said it was good to encourage personal sharing, but this group would talk about anything under the sun, and most of it pretty heavy—sex, drugs, divorce, date-rape, global warming, whether there would even be a planet in thirty years.

"What were you even doing looking under your parents' bed," Angie scolded lightly.

"Just cause you're twenty I suppose that means you're above all that sort of thing," said Sylvie mildly. "Didn't you ever look under your parents' bed?"

"Just wait till you have teenagers yourself. Then you'll be sorry you were such a brat."

"I figure we'll all be extinct before that ever happens," said Sylvie more soberly.

"I'm never getting married," said Michelle. "What's the point when you have less than fifty-fifty odds?"

"Yeah, and when most of the guys are total macho idiots," said Lin with disgust. Lin and her boyfriend had split up on the weekend.

"You guys are just way too cynical," said Angie. In many ways she agreed with them, but that wasn't what the lesson outline said. "We're supposed to be talking about hope. She looked at the purpose, which read, 'To celebrate God's hope in the Season of Lent.' Now, can any of you suggest anything hopeful in your lives or in our world?"

There was a long pause.

"There are cookies at coffee hour today," said Michelle, genuinely trying to be cooperative.

"And it's almost time to go eat them," added Sylvie. The rest of the group cheered, and Angie gave up on the lesson. Besides, she wanted to find out why Rebekah Morrison was so quiet today. She just sat there the whole time, looking totally punched out. Maybe if she let the group do an early raid on the coffee-hour cookies she'd have a chance to talk to her.

4

Changes in Women's Lives

Technological change has reshaped the world around us, changing it almost beyond recognition. It has changed not only how we do things but also the pattern of our relationships. It has brought tremendous, generation-shaking changes in women's lives.

In 1957, the year of my birth, a new vaccine was introduced in Canada. It was a four-part miracle to eliminate polio, typhoid, tetanus, and whooping cough. I received this inoculation as a child, along with a shot for smallpox. I still have a small scar on my arm. By the time my youngest child was born such immunization was so routine that I scarcely gave it a second thought as I held her on my lap to receive her first needle.

In 1927 there was an epidemic of typhoid and polio in Canada. Polio claimed or forever changed young lives. Typhoid killed with brutal swiftness. Mothers held children and infants in their arms not for inoculation but to ease their suffering or await their death. Whenever we gathered in cross-generational gatherings of women, I was aware of this vast difference in our lives. Women who are now in their eighties would have grown up and had their babies in a world where children died of diseases that are virtually non-existent in middle-class twenty-first century Canada. Of course, there are still children who die in Canada and around the world of diseases that could be prevented—tuberculosis, typhoid, and a host of others are now dispro-portionately the diseases of the poor. In the thirties, typhoid or polio could strike any woman's child.

Women and Health

The year of my birth was also the year of another significant change for Cana-dian women and their families. The year 1957 saw the start of publicly funded hospitals, followed less than a decade later by the introduction of medicare. This change affected everyone, not just women, but women in childbearing years had been especially vulnerable if they could not afford health care. In the late 1920s and early 1930s childbirth was very dangerous, especially for those without access to health care—the poor or people in rural areas. In 1928, 1,500 Canadian mothers died as a result of childbirth. Most of these deaths were due to infection and could have been prevented had the women had access to mid-wives or doctors.

Since women were, and often still are, primary caregivers for the young, the old, and the sick, the arrival of publicly funded health care had enormous implications for women's lives. Seeing a doctor or going to hospital no longer meant years of indebtedness. The burden of caring for sick relatives and neighbours was eased a little.

In 1936, 2,000 Canadian women signed a petition asking for a birth control information clinic. That same year a Canadian woman, Dorothea Palmer was charged with the illegal act of distributing birth control information to other women. In 1956, oral contraceptives were first produced amid enormous questions about availability, morality, and legality. In 1963, the first public meeting of Planned Parenthood was held, a meeting still shrouded in legal ambiguity—would participants be arrested? Was distribution of information about contraception still an illegal act? Less than a year later, birth control pills were readily available in most parts of Canada. In Toronto in 1963, the pill was issued free to any woman on welfare who wanted it. By 1988, abortion on demand was available virtually anywhere in Canada. All this, in the span of fewer than fifty years!

I entered my formative adolescent years in a context when pregnancy was, to a large degree, within a women's power to choose or not, when it was possible to be sexually active without becoming pregnant. Probably AIDS did not yet exist, and other sexually transmitted diseases were not considered a major threat. I and my generational cohort received sex education in high school and attended universities and colleges where information on sexuality and contraception were included the first-year-student information packages. Regardless of how one may feel about these changes, there is no question that my generation's attitudes to sex and sexuality were shaped by what had happened in less than half a lifetime.

And just as surely as the access to safe affordable contraception influenced my generation's approach to sexuality, AIDS has had an impact on a younger generation. The existence of AIDS was only just reaching public consciousness when I was in my twenties. By the time my oldest daughter was born, it was a fact of life and death.

Equal Rights and Work

In the area of rights, equity, and employment, the changes have also been very significant, though sometimes change has seemed like two steps forward, one step backward. Canadian women won the right to vote in federal elections in 1918, but ten years later the Supreme Court ruled that they were not "persons" under the law, and it was 1940 before women could vote in Québec. The 1920s also saw the first Canadian women admitted to the bar, but in the 1930s in some provinces women were still not allowed to practise law. In 1986 the federal Employment Equity Bill was passed to provide "equal pay for work of equal value" but in the 1990s women in the federal civil service were still fighting for pay equity.

Each landmark decision of the 1930s, 1940s, and 1950s opened up more fields of employment for women. Women were first admitted to ordained ministry in the United Church in 1936, but it was several decades before women entered that occupation in any significant numbers (or were allowed to continue working after they married!). In the years of the Second World War, many women moved into jobs that had traditionally been reserved for men. The moment the war was over, however, hundreds of thousands of women were laid off. There were other more subtle social pressures to encourage women to stay in the home rather than in the workplace. But women returned to the workforce in greater and greater numbers with each passing decade. By the 1990s, six out of every ten women were working outside the home. That is an enormous change when you consider that in 1950 fewer than a quarter of all women did. Recession, restructuring, and the disappearance of many jobs cut this back significantly later in the decade, but male employment rates fell almost as much. Unlike the post war "return home," women of the 1990s had clearly entered the workforce to stay.

Earlier in the century women typically worked outside the home until they married or had children. A significant number returned to work later, after their children had grown up. However, by the mid-1970s this pattern had begun to change. Between 1961 and 1971 the rate of employment for women who had pre-school children more than doubled (CACSW 1978). Fewer and fewer women now leave the job market after they have children. By 1994, 63 percent of women with children under sixteen and 56 percent of women with children under six worked full-time (Evans 1997, 201). Part of the reason is economic—they may be the sole wage earners or their family may be dependent on their income. Another reason is job security. They may not feel they would be able to return to the labour market if they leave for a significant period of time. Or, if they are married, their partner may not have sufficient job security for them to risk leaving the paid workforce. As well, women's sense of identity is often closely linked to their profession or vocation.

Regardless of whether women work outside the home or not, women still retain primary responsibility for housework and childcare. Housework has changed over the decades, of course, and many chores that used to take hours can now be done in minutes. But housework hasn't gone away, and women are still doing most of it. According to Statistics Canada's 1992 time-use survey, women do almost 70% of all housework. On the 1996 census, of women who work-full time and have male partners, over half reported doing fifteen or more hours of unpaid housework a week. And that's just the housework. Add in child-care—64% of women said they are doing fifteen hours or more of child care a week—and that means more than half of all women are working an additional thirty hours on top of the forty or so they may spend working and commuting. Among working men with young children, only 23% spent fifteen hours a week on housework, and 39% said they spent fifteen or more hours a week on child care.

Another way of looking a this is that on any given day, 83% of employed women spend an average of 2.25 hours on housework, compared with 50 percent of employed men who spend an average of 1.75 hours. Seventy-eight percent of women have sole responsibility for meal preparation, cleaning, and laundry, while men tend to focus on outdoor tasks and jobs that are both more discretionary and less regular (Evans 1997, 205). When women with children say they are busy and feeling stressed, it appears that they are, and disproportionately so.

Changes in working patterns for women have been accompanied by changes in attitudes and perceptions. In 1954 only about half of all Canadians thought that women who did the same work as men should receive the same pay. However, by 1985, 96% of Canadians supported the principle of equal pay for women (Bibby 1995, 57). Actual changes in women's income and employment equity, however, have not been as great as the changes in attitudes. Over the last century women's actual incomes have remained fairly constant—about 60% of men's, and the range of occupations for most women is also still very narrow—professional (mainly nursing and teaching), clerical, commercial and financial, and the service sector (Phillips and Phillips 1993, 3). For women who work full-time year-round, the gap between men's and women's incomes has closed, but only slightly. In 1976 the income of women employed full-time was 60% of men's. In 1990 the comparable figure was 67.6% (ibid.).

Another change, the so-called "feminization of poverty," has been far more significant for women. According to a 1990 study, *Women and Labour Market Poverty*, the proportion of the poor who are women rose from just under 46 percent in 1971 to almost 60 percent in 1986. (Phillips and Phillips 1993, 4). Women are now over a third more likely to be poor than men. Most vulnerable are the elderly and women who are single parents.

Feminism

Changes in women's lives over the decades are not just economic, of course. Each decade has brought different issues into public consciousness—sexuality and contraception in the 1960s, equal rights and violence against women in the 1970s, sexual harassment and sexual abuse in the 1980s, adoptive rights, surrogate rights, and child custody issues in the 1990s. Each decade has introduced different assumptions about women's rights, women's role, and women's power.

I remember when I first encountered feminism, sometime in the mid-1970s. I remember it like building blocks: little pieces of awareness and experience were piled one by one on the other. There was my first job, when I was sixteen, working in a roadside store cutting blocks of cheese and ringing in the fresh vegetables. The owner, a man with alcohol on his breath and a vicious tongue, leaned too close to me against the cash register. I knew it was not wise or safe to be alone in the store with him. With my second job, working in a hospital cafeteria when I was a sumer student, came the realization that male students earned 20 cents an hour more than the female students, for doing exactly the same work. The "dumb blond" and "woman driver" jokes began to jangle my nerves. And there were all the stories my sisters and friends told me. The blocks piled one upon the other until the tower crumbled and my world no longer looked the same.

Those building blocks of injustice against women, or ones very much like them, have been around for generations, centuries. What was different, I think, in the formative years of my generation, was that the stories were told. The blocks were labelled, put on display for all to see. The violence was hidden no longer. The unspoken assumptions about women's place and the quiet injustices of daily work and pay were all out in the open. The experiences were analysed: sexism, patriarchy, misogyny were named and understood as the underlying factors. We talked about it. We changed our assumptions, changed the words, challenged the pay scales, and questioned the balance sheet.

Of course, all this was happening within the lifetime and experience of older women too. Some of them embraced this awareness and started changing the words of hymns, teaching husbands to cook, and claiming rights previously unheard of. My own generation wasn't uniformly "consciousness-raised" either, and many resisted the changes in roles and in understanding. But, I believe that something happened in this process that was different for my generation than for previous ones. It was different because all of this came to a head in our formative years. It created a common bond for those of us who lived through those times.

I find it hard to imagine a time before medicare or childhood inoculations, and have no real sense of what it might have been like to grow up in the years of war and depression. It may also be hard for women significantly older or younger than me to understand how significant it was for me when the CUPE union contract at the hospital where I worked eventually had the same pay scale for women and men doing the same job. But there is a gap at the other end of the generation continuum as well. Just as I cannot really understand what it must have been like for women to have no access to contraception, I cannot fully grasp what it is like to reach sexual maturity in a world where AIDS exists.

A Chronology of Events for Women in the Twentieth Century

Up to 1918   Women's movement was concerned with such issues as temperance, poverty, health, and prostitution, and later concerned about peace issues and women's right to vote.

1918   Women in Canada are granted the right to vote in federal elections.

1920   Women are allowed to stand for federal election.

1921   Canada's first female member of parliament, Agnes MacPhail, is elected.

1928   Canadian Supreme Court rules that women are not persons. This ruling is appealed to and overturned by the British Privy Council a year later, paving the way for women to be appointed senators.

1930   Canada's first female senator, Cairine Wilson, is appointed.

1936   Dorothea Palmer is charged with distributing birth control information.

1940   Women obtain the right to vote in provincial elections in Québec (the last province to grant this).

1944   The Family Allowance, or "baby bonus," becomes Canada's first universal welfare program paid monthly to families with children to help cover the costs of child maintenance. For many women it was often the first time they had money of their own to use for their children's benefit.

1948   Canada signs the Universal Declaration of Human Rights adopted by the United Nations General Assembly. The Declaration includes protection of human rights regardless of sex.

1955   Rosa Parks makes history by refusing to give up her bus seat at the front (reserved for whites) in Montgomery, Alabama.

1956   The contraceptive pill is produced. It becomes readily available in the early 1960s.

1960   The Voice of Women is formed to work for world peace.

1960   Mrs. Bandaranaike of Sri Lanka becomes first elected woman prime minister in the world.

1963   The first public meeting of Planned Parenthood is held.

1968   Canada's first unified divorce law is passed, making divorces much easier to obtain.

1970	Report of the Royal Commission on the Status of Women in Canada. The 167 recommendations in areas of federal responsibility "focused attention on women's grievances, recommended changes to eliminate sexual inequality by means of social policy, and moblized a constituency of women's groups to press for implementation of the commission's recommendations." (*The Canadian Encyclopedia* 1988, 1756)
1971	Statistics Canada recognizes household work as a significant contributor to Canada's Gross Domestic Product (GDP), estimating that housework represents 41% of the GDP.
1971	Women are given the vote in Switzerland (some cantons still do not give women voting rights, however).
1975	The International Year for Women. The United Nations holds its first women's conference in Mexico City.
1976	The United Nations begins the Decade for Women (1976–1985)
1980	Second World Conference for the United Nations Decade for Women, in Copenhagen, adopts a plan of action to promote the status of women throughout the second half of the UN Decade.
1982	The first woman judge, Bertha Wilson, is appointed to the Canadian Supreme Court
1984	The report of the Royal Commission on Employment Equity is received. This highlights the concept of employment equity. The Employment Equity Bill is introduced in 1986.
1985	The Indian Act is amended, allowing aboriginal women who marry non-status men to retain their status (prior to this, men who married non-status women did not lose their status but women did).
1989	On December 6, fourteen women engineering students at École Polytechnique in Montréal are murdered.
1992	Roberta Bondar becomes Canada's first woman in space.
1993	Catherine Callbeck is the first Canadian women to be elected premier, in Prince Edward Island.
1993	The report of the Canadian Panel on Violence Against Women is released, highlighting concerns about women and violence.
1997	Mother Teresa, who dedicated her life to serving the poor in India, dies at aged 87.

5

Frameworks

The world has changed to an extent that many of us still find hard to comprehend, but there is something else operating in the generation gap. Not only have women of different generations inhabited a different world, they have also looked out on the world from a very different frame of reference. They see reality differently because they don't look at things with the same eyes. It isn't just that I don't know what is going on in the world of previous or subsequent generations, it is also that my way of looking at the world is different.

There is considerable evidence that we view the world through filters formed from our experiences. Our experience and our socialization set up a kind of selective screening process through which we come to view reality. In other words, when we look at the world around us, we see only what we have learned to see. Human beings all do this to simplify a complex world; we view things in categories. This process of ordering and organizing reality into concepts and categories is a psychological necessity. We need to see a cat as part of the general category of "cats," for example, to avoid being totally overwhelmed by each new piece of data that enters our view. However, these categories inevitably intrude between us and the world outside us. According to Douglas Walrath, author of *Frameworks*, each of us has a "framework" shaped by our accumulated psychological, social, and cultural experiences. Walrath demonstrates that "over time, as we perceive the world repeatedly through our own filters, each of us builds up a personal frame of reference that forms our perceptual 'framework'" (1987, 4).

Frameworks and Culture

Frameworks are not just for individuals. Cultures and societies also have distinct frameworks. What we perceive and believe about the world around us is a complex interaction between the framework developed within our culture and what is out there in the so-called real world. When we share a culture we all believe in what we all see.

Here's an example of how frameworks shape perception. When I look at the moon I often see a face there. That's typical of our culture. We have been taught to "see" the "man in the moon" and so we do. When I travelled to Zambia, I discovered that Zambians see a "rabbit in the moon." We look at the same moon with the same shapes. Viewed from one perspective it's a face; from another, it's a rabbit. I never saw the rabbit before, but having been introduced to it, now I see it all the time. All I have to do is tilt my head to the Zambian point of view, and there it is! Frameworks are like that. We take for granted our way of seeing reality until we encounter a different way of looking at the same thing. We can discard or discount the other perspective, or we can start to look at reality differently.

All of us probably have had experiences within our multicultural society of how different our cultures are, and how sometimes that really does affect how we view so-called reality. When two different cultures interact, different views of reality may also rub against each other.

Here's another example. In Zambia I had occasion to work with rural women's organizations involved in small economic ventures in their communities. I participated in a training workshop with these women—a workshop aimed at helping these organizations develop management skills. There was a presentation on record-keeping and group management. The presenter was trying to impress upon the group the importance of accurate bookkeeping and minute-taking. At one point in the process he did a little exercise with the group. He sent three women out of the room, and told the rest of the group the story of *Goldilocks and the Three Bears*; actually he told it as *Braided Hair and the Three Elephants*, but it was essentially the same story, a story unknown to the group. He asked one of the women outside to come back, and invited someone from the group to tell the story to her. She did so, getting many of the details wrong. Then he asked the woman who had most recently returned to call back one of the women still outside and tell her the story. Of course, each time the story was told details were lost or changed. His point was that you have to write it down or you'll forget it.

A little later in the session, however, an older woman on the group stood up. She was the oldest woman in the group, small and bent over. Her name was Loveness. She was the bookkeeper for her group. Loveness was illiterate, but used a traditional system for keeping the financial records. She stood up to tell the group a story and the story she told was *Braided Hair and the Three Elephants*. She did so in a traditional, full-bodied storytelling style. One could practically feel those elephants in the room with us. And she told the story without missing a single detail—the sequence was accurate, the parts of the story were all there. Her point, she said, was that you have to learn to listen!

For me this was an epiphany moment—a sudden realization of how different cultural frameworks can be from each other. Until Loveness told her story and presented her moral lesson to the group, I had totally taken for granted the assumption the presenter was making. If you want an accurate record of something, write it down. That's my Western world view. But Loveness knew that records can get lost or destroyed, and that many people can't read, and that pens and paper aren't easy to come by in rural Zambia. Her culture had taught her that if you want an accurate record of something, store it in a really safe place—give it to the storyteller! Since then I have become increasingly aware of how cultures have their own frames of reference: each may be incomprehensible to the other; each is perfectly valid in its own context.

Frameworks and Generations

What may be less apparent is that generations also have their own distinct frameworks. What we see or understand appears different depending on our framework. In the same way that cultures differ in their way of seeing the world, so too, do age groups.

It used to be that everyone in a given society grew up in essentially the "same world." Members of each generation would have had the same framework, because they were raised in the same society. That is no longer the case. The younger generation is growing up in a different world. The older generation inhabits a different time and also, therefore, a different culture. Each generation to some extent lacks the categories necessary to understand the framework of the other. Each generation understands best, or perhaps *only* understands, its own cohort—its own generational compatriots.

Each generation is shaped distinctly by the major social events that happen during the formative years of socialization. When youth move from their family homes out into the culture that surrounds them, they are shaped by what is going on in that culture. When adolescents move into a different environment they take on the shape of that culture; adults don't do so to nearly the same degree. According to Karl Mannheim, one of the key social scientists to develop this theory, adolescence is the critical age for this acculturation to happen—roughly the years from ages of thirteen to twenty-two. This is the crucial time, just as the young person is moving out into the world but before the process of acculturation becomes more fixed or solidified (Walrath 1987, 31–32).

"When these fundamental years of acculturation to the larger world take place amid social crisis and upheaval, our fundamental picture of the world is shaped by these crises," says Douglas Walrath (33). The crises destabilize us, and forever after we share a bond with those who were similarly destabilized. Walrath agrees that ages from thirteen to twenty-two are the critical years within which a generation's culture is shaped.

Think for a moment about what was going on in the world around you during the years you were thirteen to twenty-two. As you reflect on the major events or circumstances, you may notice things that shaped your own generation, setting it apart from others. You may be find that you share a bond of common understanding with those who grew up facing a second world war in less than half a century. Or the Depression of the 1930s may have forever shaped your view of plenty and scarcity. Perhaps a famine or war in your homeland may have resulted in major dislocation, forever shaping your outlook on the world.

If you were a member of a generation growing up with the recession of the 1980s or growing consciousness of the potential destruction of the earth's environment, you may view the earth as more finite and limited than those who were socialized in the "limitless" years of opportunity and optimism of the 1950s and 1960s. If you learned how to survive as a young adult in amid scarcity, famine, rationing, widespread unemployment, or war, you may look askance at the wastefulness or confidence those who have never known scarcity.

Obviously the personal events that take place in the life of each individual are also important, but this theory makes the additional claim that critical social events can shape a whole generation's outlook. For example, the generation that spent its formative years during the Depression or the Second World War was shaped or influenced differently from the generation that spent its formative years in the boom times of the 1950s or the social upheaval and crisis years of the 1960s and 1970s. To give a personal example, from someone whose framework was shaped in Canada during the late 1960s and early 1970s—change for me is normal and to be expected. I take completely for granted the fact that change does and will occur, because it has always been part of my world. Also because of what was going on in society at that time— the civil rights movement, formation of student organizations on university campuses, the beginning of the modern women's movement, coalitions to end the Vietnam war—I also tend to expect that I/we can control and influence change. I view the world through this lens, to some degree—change is a fact of life, change is positive and moves us forward, change can be influenced or directed by people working together.

For someone whose formative years were the Second World War–years in Europe or Canada, change may be viewed not as normal or natural but as an aberration. The changes that happened in her world—Depression followed by devastating war—were neither positive nor controllable. In her life experience, the world was soon going to return to "the way things were." For her, change may be anything but "normal" and certainly not positive. These generational frameworks, while they obviously do not define all of who we are, can sometimes block understanding and communication across generations.

Put people from these two different frameworks on a church committee dealing with issues of change, for example, or ask them to discuss changes to the structure of women's organizations, and they may respond very differently. One woman, operating from one generational framework may be much more cautious about change, much more anxious to preserve what is good and valuable, and may see the other as wanting to change for the sake of change. The other, from another generation, may view change as both good and necessary, and may feel impatient with what she perceives as unnecessary caution or conservatism.

Generational Cohorts

Walrath describes three distinct generational cohorts in North America. Each cohort has a distinctly different framework. Walrath calls these three cohorts by the names Strivers, Challengers, and Calculators.

Strivers were born between 1901 and 1931. Their key formative years (the years when they were thirteen to twenty-two) were 1914 to 1953, years of war and economic depression.

Challengers were born between 1932 and 1954. Their generation's formative years—from 1945 to 1976—started in a time of victory celebrations, economic affluence and general optimism, but by the time of the last of the Challengers reached adulthood, the world was also facing the beginnings of economic and cultural cutbacks and recession.

Calculators were born after 1955. Their period of cultural formation took place after 1968. They reached adulthood in a context of environmental concerns, job scarcity, economic recession, and limited resources. Since Walrath did his analysis in the late 1980s, we would probably now add a forth cohort—those women who are now in their teens and early twenties, what David Foot (1996) calls the "echo" generation, so named because these children of the baby boomers have produced a small blip or echo on demographic charts.

Walrath did extensive interviews to identify the key formative events for each generation, as well as the characteristics shared by each.

For the Strivers, whose world was shaken by wars and depression, stability is the norm and change is the aberration. Strivers are survivors who have lived through very difficult times. They value loyalty, duty, obligation, and hard work. Even after the crises that prompted these responses have passed, many Strivers keep on "striving," perhaps out of a need to protect their society and themselves from future catastrophe. Just as they waited for the unwelcome changes of war or economic depression to end, they tend to view other unwelcome changes as something to outlast or resist, until things "return to normal."

Strivers grew up watching parents who, for the most part, struggled hard just to survive; on farms or in factories daily life was an endless round of very hard work. Strivers learned how to work hard themselves, as they struggled with the adversities of war or depression. My own parents, of the Striver generation, have many stories to tell of such hard work, from the efforts of their families to put food on the table during the war, to the years when, from the age of fourteen on, they worked full time to help support themselves or their extended families.

The Challengers, that massive baby boom generation, challenged the traditional social order and developed their own generational identity and culture, often in radical opposition to the generations before them. The sheer size of the baby boom generation had an impact on how this generation thinks about the world and about themselves. They grew up expecting to be able to make changes, both personally and collectively.

Technological changes, oral contraceptives, and, in the US, the civil rights movement and Vietnam all ensured that their world and their world view would be very different from those of their parents. The Challengers grew up in a world in flux, a world with the looming threat of nuclear war. Upheaval and change are the norm for this generation. As Walrath describes it, to be socialized in a segmented world means that you have a permanent sense of uprootedness. This is the reality for all but the generation of the Strivers. In spite of this sense of being uprooted, Challengers tend to be a very optimistic cohort, because most were socialized in optimistic, forward-looking, post-war economic boom times.

Calculators came along at the tail end of or just after the baby boom. They experienced the cutbacks and loss of opportunity that followed the big boom. Schools closed, universities had no places, teaching jobs disappeared, *all* jobs dried up as the massive baby boom cohort moved through, snapping up all the spaces and opportunities, leaving in its wake a much smaller and somewhat disappointed generation. This is a generation that knows the limits of the world's resources. They do not share the sense of unlimited possibilities of the previous generation. They know that, in a world of cutbacks and constraints, to survive one has to calculate, to make careful choices, to conserve and preserve. For Calculators, change is normal, but they don't view it so positively as the Challengers. Change may be normal, but so are cutbacks, limits, depleted resources, downsizing, and unemployment. Change is a given, but it isn't necessarily such a good thing.

There are some limits to this theory. A generational framework is a description of a mindset or way of apprehending the world. It is not a description of values or beliefs. For example, someone who comes from a generation for which change is both positive and normal might tend to see herself as an agent of change. Her perspective might be: "I have the power to make changes; I can change this for the better." However, this says nothing about the values she holds or the kind of change that she supports. Change might be focused on the self or it might be altruistic. It might be directed towards technological progress or world peace, getting ahead in the world or ending poverty.

People might challenge the notion of frameworks by arguing that "I know women in their eighties who are strong feminists and women in their thirties who are opposed to feminism." But the theory of frameworks doesn't say anything about these kinds of values. Of course there have been people who have worked for justice for women for many decades, for example, those who fought for the vote for women.

There is a further limitation on the theory of frameworks. People may for example, know of people who are of the Strivers age group who think and act much more like Challengers, in how they apprehend the world. A generational framework, once it exists, is also available to members of all previous generations who can and may adopt it. It would be an extreme over-generalization to say that all people of a given generation hold onto their generation's framework for a lifetime. Most do, but many don't. Most of those in a generation raised in the Depression and war years may view change as bad and not normal (we'll soon get back to the way things were). They may act out this framework on a church committee, for example. Or, as Strivers, they may always be preparing for some future catastrophe or famine. But some within their own generation may have adopted the framework of subsequent generations (the optimism of the 1950s generation, for example) or the proactive, change-initiating framework of the 1960s crowd.

And there is a final limitation on this theory of generational frameworks. Walrath's analysis and data collection, while very extensive, all took place in the United States. It applies in only general terms to Canadians, and even less to those who reached adulthood outside of North America. Cultural differences add their own layers of difference. Someone may have been socialized within a "Challenger" generation in North America, but if they reached adulthood very isolated from others in their generation they may have been less influenced by the larger social trends. One of the questions I wondered about as I began the workshop process was to what extent one can make generalizations about these groups of Strivers, Challengers, Calculators, and the Echo cohort. Are Strivers the same in rural PEI as they are in suburban Ontario or urban Alberta?

I began by asking women themselves to name what they thought were the key "generation shaping events" in their society or their world, for their age-group, and then to identify what they felt was the impact of these events on the world view of their generation.

Generational Groupings

Generation	Born in...	Years of socialization...	Affected by...
Strivers	1901 to 1931	1914 to 1953	economic Depression and war
Challengers	1932 to 1954	1945 to 1976	end of war, affluence and optimism, social change movements, then cutbacks and recession
Calculators	1955 to 1975	1968 to 1988	environmental concerns, job scarcity, economic recession, limited resources
Echo generation	after 1975	1988 to present	technological change, insecurity, cutbacks, environmental crises

6

Women's Frames of Reference

In the Naomi's Daughters workshops we gathered around a timeline of major historical changes and events. Using the timeline as a catalyst, members of each age group talked about the circumstances that shaped their generation of women. I introduced the concept of key formative events shaping generational frameworks to explore how frameworks have shaped our relationships as women in the church. I asked two questions:

- What key historical or social events occurred during the time when you were aged thirteen to twenty-two that shaped the lives of women in your generation?
- How do you think your generation of women was influenced or affected by these events?

As each generation spoke of their experiences, I found that there were distinct parallels with the generational categories that Douglas Walrath used, so I have continued to use his terms to describe those three age groups.

Strivers: Surviving Depression and War

Douglas Walrath categorizes the Strivers as people born before 1932. These are women who were aged sixty-eight or older in 2000. Strivers made up about a third of the participants in the Naomi's Daughters workshops. Most were at the younger end of this cohort, women in their late sixties and early seventies, although a few were women well into their eighties. In spite of this relatively wide age span, the Strivers in the workshops seemed to have the greatest sense of commonality as a generation and used the fewest words to describe the pivotal experiences of their formative years. "The Depression" and "Second World War"—these words were sufficient to sum up what had shaped their generation.

These were the two great events that together transformed the world for this group of Canadian women. The shattering devastation that began with the collapse of the stock market in 1929 continued through years of drought and unemployment in the 1930s, and ended in war.

The effects of the Depression were vast. It is estimated that, by 1937, over one-and-a-half million Canadians were without employment. Most women in the workshops recalled the hardships faced by their own families; even if they were very young during the years before the war, they were keenly aware of what their parents had experienced. "We didn't waste anything," they said. "We had large gardens to feed the family for the winter." "We discovered that you don't need everything you think you need."

Even women whose families were more affluent felt the impact, and no one could avoid the devastating poverty felt by the most vulnerable in their communities. One woman summed the images that became imbedded in her mind, "It was the people we saw begging in the streets." The church, at the centre of the lives of most communities, was very involved in distribution of goods, charity, used clothing. Of course, women were pivotal to those activities with the church.

Then, in 1939, Canada declared war, and another devastating change hit their communities. "The war shaped our days," said one woman, as she recalled the daily ritual of listening to the radio news and the announcements of friends, family members, or local people who had been killed. Many women remembered watching the war documentaries at the Saturday matinee: the looming crisis of war on the horizon, the annexation of Austria, Canada's declaration of war, and the scenes of troop movements and battlefields, all in black and white on the big screen.

War wasn't just on the big screen, however. "War changed the face of Ottawa," said one woman who had lived in Ottawa all her life. It changed the face of many other communities and it changed the lives of women and their families.

With war came more hardships, as rationing and shortages extended even into the middle class. Women recalled the large "war gardens" planted to keep families fed through the winter, canning the harvest—three to four hundred jars of fruit and vegetables every fall. Butter rationing was particularly significant. Butter, or lack thereof, became a symbol of something much larger—a symbol of prosperity, a sign of these terrible times, and a reminder of life as it was "before" when butter was plentiful.

"Fear" was another word that women of this generation used often. Through all those years there was the fear of what might happen, fear for who might be next on the list of killed or missing, fear evoked by the daily struggle to survive. Fear was the backdrop behind every daily event.

Extended families and the community became particularly important for survival in the Depression and war years. The experience of several generations living under the same roof was very common for this generation as they were growing up. Community was important. "We had to care for each other," explained a woman from the Maritimes. "We were kind of thrown together by these events and we became more responsible. We became more conscious of others. We lived as a community."

The war had enormous implications not only for women's role in their homes, farms, and families, but also for their involvement in the wider society. Before the war the predominant expectation was that girls would marry soon after high school. Most women married young and there were few expectations or opportunities to do anything else. Most women weren't expected to go to university, and there were few fields of employment into which women would be readily accepted.

When war was declared, women were suddenly called out into the wider society. They were encouraged to enter the factories and other fields of employment traditionally reserved for men. Women were doing jobs they had never done before, and the media were full of stories about how well the women were doing these new things and how much the war effort needed them. The war brought women out of the home and into the workplace.

"I think it brought about a revolution in home life," said one woman from the rural Prairies, now in her late seventies. "After women had been out there in the world, they were never entirely satisfied to be in the home."

War was a great teacher. "It taught us to flow with the times," was the way one woman expressed it. Women learned to drive cars, to operate machinery. Many now had independent incomes and often were heads of their household while their men folk were away. One woman in rural Ontario characterized the change this way: "Women learned to make decisions for themselves, to be independent in raising their families. They had to learn how to handle money."

Women talked about how their generation was shaped by these events and changes. "We were a whole generation raised to think about how you spend your money. My dad never owned a house. He couldn't take on debt. In the Depression he saw people lose everything. He couldn't face that."

"We tend to be very security-minded, always saving for a rainy day," said one woman, and another, who grew up in the Depression, added, "I still have the saving and economizing mindset." Women used words like "frugal" to describe a generation that learned to cope with many hardships. They had learned to save, to scrimp, to do without, to cut corners, to adapt, to make do, and to make something from nothing.

This survival mentality was a characteristic of women from the Striver's generation, and it came through clearly in all the workshops. Women talked about hard work and determined effort, responsibility, duty and obligation— all of which they still value very highly. These characteristics seemed to transcend differences in values and beliefs, a set of qualities that overrode individual differences.

For example, some women talked about their pride in the war effort. "We were the last generation that went to war to protect our country," said one. For her, the war reinforced a strong sense of patriotism. "The world was divided into good guys and bad guys. We of course thought we were the good guys," said one woman who lost her high school sweetheart when his fighter aircraft crashed. Other women came out of the war with very different attitudes. "I became a strong pacifist," explained one. "I was very influenced by the fact that a whole generation of young men went to war and never came back."

Women also had very different opinions about women's changing role. After the war women had independence and, often, paid jobs, which allowed them more freedom. Most women agreed on these facts, but not on the implications. For some this was a good thing, while others blamed this new-found freedom for rising divorce rates and the breakup of the family.

Although attitudes to particular changes were very different, the overall framework for looking at change itself was very consistent across this age group. "It was very much our expectation that this was the 'war to end all wars' and that after the war things would go back to normal," said one woman. Time and again, this cohort referred to "getting back to normal" as an operational mindset. Even when some of the vast social changes wrought by Depression or war, such as greater independences for women, were welcomed, this generation of women still tended to view change as something outside of the norm.

Change may happen; stability is still the predominant expectation. Thus women of this generation may have become strong pacifists not to "change the status quo" (as in the anti-Vietnam era) but to protect what is of value, to defend peace, or to preserve the life of communities, families, and societies. Or they may become strong nationalists and defenders of the war effort out of the same operational framework—resistance to changes such as the devastating changes that their generation was forced to survive. This urge to protect, to sustain, to conserve when faced with change seems to be a predominant generational quality.

This doesn't mean that this generation is universally resistant or opposed to all change, or that it is inherently more conservative than other generations. I met many women in this age group who were strong feminists or advocates of women's rights, and many who had undergone enormous changes in their own attitudes to such things as sexuality, politics, religion, economics, or global justice. Perhaps more than any other generation, this is a group that has learned how to cope with change and how to survive it. I met women now in their eighties who know how to "keep up" and will learn to use computers if they have to in order to do so. I met many women who over the years have consistently participated in study groups to keep current on world affairs and learn about justice issues. I suspect this age group may know more about many United Church mission and justice themes than most other generational groupings.

The Second World War opened up the world for many women. Often it brought contact with people from other nations, cultures, and lifestyles. This was a generation plunged into the wider world as events that were happening thousands of miles away had a direct and daily impact. These are women who have had to be flexible enough to adapt to the enormous change that swept the world.

However, in spite of, or perhaps because of, the great changes that they experienced, there is, in this age group, a fundamental difference in their approach to change. It is this difference that sets them apart from the generations that came after them. In their lives, change is an outsider. Welcome or not, change is still a stranger on the doorstep. Unlike all the generations that come after them, they remember a time when change was not an omnipresent facet of daily life. They have survived the winds of change that blew in with such ferocity in the years of Depression and war, but they know there was a time "before all that" when daily life did not change all that much.

Challengers: From Stability to Social Upheaval

Walrath describes the Challenges as those born between 1932 and 1954, that is, women who would be in their mid-forties to late sixties in 2000. The pivotal events for this generation began not with war but with the ending of war. Women at the oldest end of the Challenger cohort remember the troop trains returning, the uniforms everywhere, and the dancing in the streets. The outpouring of jubilation that spilled onto the Canadian streets when the war ended is an event this generation of women recalls vividly. This, the ending of the war, was seen by many as the event that shaped their generation.

The years immediately after the war were times of relative stability and economic prosperity. Things did indeed seem to go back to normal. Like those of the Striver generation before them, the older women in the Challenger group use the language of normalcy to describe what was happening. Statements like this were typical of what I heard from this group in the workshops: "The war was just over and the country was getting back to normal."

The post-war years were a time of economic growth and prosperity for many in Canada. Women from all parts of the country noted that there were lots of jobs. "It never crossed our minds that we wouldn't get a job," said the women. Jobs were permanent in those days or, for women, until marriage. Job security for most men, however, was a given.

The era ushered in a new availability of consumer goods. "Things started to boom. We had things we didn't have before and we were able to do things we couldn't do before." Compared to the war years, these were indeed times of plenty for many in Canada.

This time of transition from war to the post-war years of stability and economic security was not just a "return to normal" however. There were changes in many areas of life. In the early fifties Canada was becoming more industrialized, and technological change was afoot. Depending on where women lived, the technological changes happened at different times, but the general trend was apparent everywhere. Women in the workshops noted the shift from horses to cars or the introduction of electricity and running water into their homes, the building of a highway or their first encounter with TV.

With industrialization in Canada came greater urbanization. Some women moved to the cities to find work. With increasingly efficient transportation and better roads came the centralization of schools. Many women recalled the one-room schoolhouses of their parents being replaced by larger regional schools.

After the war, there was significant pressure to move women back into the home. Some women recall this as a positive thing, part of the "return to normal." One woman said, "Women were bumped back into the home, but I didn't feel this as negative." Others however, decried the change. "After the war women were told by society and the church to go back home. We had to fight to save daycares and it was a bit of a losing battle."

Young women entering adulthood in the fifties certainly did have more freedom, more choices, and had more formal education than their mothers and grandmothers. But as one woman describes it, "Women were still limited in what they were expected to be able to do. I was expected to get an education, with the choices of nurse, teacher, or secretary." These certainly were the main career options for women. The big three—teaching, nursing, and secretarial work—were mentioned consistently by women from rural PEI to urban Edmonton. And, of course, women got married. "There was lots of stigma for women who didn't marry. Get a job, but only for three or four years, then you get married."

The post-war years shaped this generation's outlook on the world very differently from those socialized amid the crises of Depression and war. The experience of the war seemed to open up the world view of the Strivers. Post-war security and the strong drive to return to normal seemed to close it down for the next generation. Time and again in the workshops, women who experienced adolescence in the 1950s recall "not really noticing much of what was going on in the wider world."

One woman described it this way, "This was the plastic fifties. I think we were largely insulated from world events." This sense of being somehow isolated or removed from the outside world was a common trait, experienced by many women in this age group regardless of location. Women in rural areas said things like "We weren't as aware of world events. It was happening 'out there,' but things that were closer to home affected people more." Others from urban areas said things like "We were a self-centred group, maybe not as aware as previous generations." This is the group who, when asked what was going on in the world during their adolescent years very often answered with phrases like, "I really wasn't all that aware of much going on outside my immediate family or community" or simply mentioned the local events—the dances, the parties, high school, family, first jobs. One women summed it up this way, "Ours was the generation that turned inward. The war was over. All of us seemed to live in 'our own little world.' I don't have any sense of hearing world news."

Within every workshop, there seemed to be a sub-group of "women of the fifties" who viewed the world from the secure, safe, and prosperous lens of post-war Canada. "We were a hopeful people, and very secure," they said of themselves. "The future was going to be okay. We danced and laughed. We believed we could make a difference." This generation was raised in an oasis of calm, when compared to the war years and the turbulence to come. The predominant values of the time included the importance of education, security, and hard work. "Behave yourself and you'll do fine," was how one woman described the prevailing attitudes to authority.

"Male dominance and religious dominance," were mentioned by others as ways of pointing to the authority structures that predominated. And on the larger landscape, the British Empire was still strong. As women noted, "most of the map was still pink." In other words, most of the world was still under the umbrella of the Commonwealth, which map-makers coloured pink. Life still centred in the community—school, church, and family. You bought only what you could pay for. Close-knit extended families were still the norm, particularly in rural areas. These are some of the words women used to describe this generation's sense of itself—conventional, secure, normalized, confident.

In my opinion, there are really two groups of Challengers. Those whose primary years of acculturation centred around the fifties, and those a little later who entered adolescence and adulthood from the mid-sixties on. The earlier group are much more positive about the world around them. They were raised in an era of affluence, stability, and relative prosperity. Even those raised in less affluent situations or very remote communities reflected this prevailing sense of optimism. Things, even if they weren't great right now, would certainly be getting better very soon. The world, viewed from the optimistic fifties, was going to be just fine.

The only clouds on the horizon these women mentioned were the Korean war and the nuclear build-up. The two were linked by a single threat, "Communism." The anti-communist hunts and trials of the McCarthy era began around the time of the Korean War, in the early 1950s. Britain and the US were doing extensive atomic testing and, in 1953, the Distant Early Warning Line (the DEW Line) was built. This string of radar stations across Canada's high arctic was intended to provide a first line of defence in the event of a Russian nuclear attack.

The construction of the DEW line was coupled with the forced relocation of many Inuit communities in a destructive and failed bid to populate the arctic. Such was the intensity of fear (and racism) that entire communities were destroyed (in some cases people literally starved to death because they had been moved into areas that could not sustain human habitation) to protect against the communist threat. But even when they mentioned these early signs of the Cold War, women whose socialization happened in the fifties did so with a sense of being largely removed from the global arena. Even the air raid drills and practising hiding under the desks at school in the event of a nuclear attack didn't really seem to upset the calm of the era. One woman recalled that her mother bought powdered milk for a while to avoid drinking in radiation from above-ground testing, and many mothers said, "don't eat snow" because of nuclear tests. That may have been happening "out there" but for the most part this generation felt remarkably sheltered.

I noticed in the workshops a marked difference between this group of women and women just a few years younger, all of whom were in the cohort defined by Walrath as Challengers. Women whose socialization happened in the sixties and seventies seem to view the world "out there" very differently. When I asked these slightly younger women what was going on in the world around them during their years of acculturation, I got a much longer list: civil rights movements, Martin Luther King, and the March on Washington; South Africa; women's rights; bombings by the FLQ [Front de Libération du Québec]; South Africa, race issues, and segregation of schools; the Cold War; the Vietnam War; the birth control pill and what some women referred to as "free love and the sexual revolution"; Castro, the Bay of Pigs, and the Cuban missile crisis. The list goes on. The turbulent sixties had begun!

The changes in technology continued apace, of course. Again, different regions were affected at different times by particular changes. In some places, it was the replacement of local telephone operators and party lines with a more private telephone system. "We didn't know what the neighbours were doing anymore." In the 1960s, TV entered many more homes. Rural electrification and indoor plumbing, which had been a fact of life for decades in some areas, now touched the lives of many more Canadians.

Communications technology was becoming more important. Cars were faster and bigger. The space race was on, culminating in the first moonwalk in 1969. The completion of the Trans-Canada Highway in 1970 changed the face of rural PEI. Communications technology was becoming more important, said women from urban areas. Whatever the particular technology, from computers to the space race, it's clear that women of this cohort were more immersed in a world of technological change than women a decade older. But for this generation changes in technology paled in comparison to the vast changes in the social landscape.

The changes in society seemed to leave no corner of Canada untouched. The women of rural PEI thought of themselves as relatively isolated. They in fact used words like "a hundred years behind" to describe how they saw themselves in relation to those in other parts of the country. This may well have been true in terms of things like rural electrification, the move from horses to cars, the building of highways or telephone exchanges (although a hundred years is a *slight* exaggeration). But what surprised me most as I listened to their conversation, and their description of their own generation, was how very much in synch these women were with their generational cohorts in other places. It may be true, as they claimed, that "Island culture is different; we're not as affected by outside events." However, the events the PEI "women of the sixties" listed as having a impact was strikingly similar to lists of events mentioned by women elsewhere in Canada.

For example, the PEI women matched the oldest group of Challengers in their description of themselves as isolated or unaffected by outside events. But the younger Challengers among the PEI women talked about how they were very much affected by things like the Vietnam War. Draft dodgers came to PEI as they did to other parts of Canada), the DEW line (many PEI folk worked to help build and staff it), and even the things such as "the sexual revolution and flower power." Even environmental issues made the list of things they were aware of in the 1960s in PEI.

Many women in this age group, right throughout the country, mentioned the civil rights movement and, in particular, the death of Martin Luther King, as a pivotal event for their generation. One woman described this way. "It had a huge impact. Somehow this event reminded us there was evil in the world." Some women saw the struggle for racial equality as a process somewhat removed from their immediate lives, something going on in the US. It may be that events like King's assassination grabbed the headlines, but this struggle also had its Canadian dimension. School segregation was outlawed in Ontario around the same time (1964) when Leonard Baithwaite, the first black Canadian elected to a provincial legislature, blasted this discriminatory law. And many women in this age group recalled the riots and racial protests in Montreal in 1969 that centred on the campus of Sir George Williams University [now Concordia].

Growing consciousness of racial injustice and inequality, while sometimes perceived as not really an issue in Canada had an impact on the Canadian social landscape. One woman pointed to the discovery that even here "black students experienced problems of racism, lack of freedom, and inequality."

The Vietnam War was also a landmark for women of this generation. Many recalled the deaths of student protestors at Kent State University in Ohio or the arrival of US draft dodgers; these were "the ones from away who stood out because they dressed differently." The peace movement moved into Canadian universities, and demonstrations happened not just in Washington but on Parliament Hill or on the campus of the University of Toronto.

Many of the social changes of the sixties and early seventies had a particular impact on women. More and more women were working outside the home. Divorce was somewhat more accepted, and a great deal more common after the new divorce law passed in 1968. The women's movement played an increasingly significant role during the early seventies. Statements like this one—"I travelled Europe extensively before going to university"—typified a whole new generation of women. In the fifties, women were still unlikely to go to university, and many would have been discouraged from doing so by their families or social convention. By the sixties, this was very much the norm. In many cases, it was the expectation. And many women tested the wings of independence with trips abroad. Changing dress codes said a lot about women's changing perceptions of themselves. The ultra-femininity of the fifties was replaced by a look that suggested independence, defiance, or outright revolt. As one participant put it, "In the late sixties and early seventies, girls said, 'we want to wear slacks,' and we did."

According to women who reached maturity in the 1950s, "sexuality outside of marriage 'happened' but it really wasn't an option." The sixties and the availability of oral contraceptives ushered in a time that some women characterized as one of new sexual freedom.

"Social conventions were gone," said one woman very bluntly. "Marriage wasn't the same. People could be anything they wanted. This was a time of very unconventional thinking. It was much more liberal." Her sentiments were echoed by many others. Something changed in the sixties, not just in the external events of the world, but in the way people felt, thought, acted, believed.

This was still a time of relative economic security, marked by confidence in availability of consumer goods, economic progress, and plenty of jobs. "There were jobs. We never even thought about not getting a job," said these women, sounding like the fifties crowd, except that the range of possible job options for women had opened up somewhat. Continuing to work after marriage and children also was much more of a possibility. There were a growing number of two-income families. "We saw a big difference between our lifestyle and our mothers' lifestyle. Most of our mothers didn't work outside the home," said some.

That kind of statement was very typical of the women socialized in the sixties. That kind of differentiation came up often in the workshops, but only from this generation on. Although one would not be able to pinpoint an exact date and time, and the timing may well be different from place to place, something happened in this era that set this generation apart. They needed to say, "we are different from our mothers." Previous generations didn't seem to say it so explicitly. I'm sure if they were asked they would point out the many ways in which they and their lives were different from their mothers, but that's not quite what I mean. It's as though at a certain point a generation appeared that needed to mark, to claim the difference. And claim it they did, much more sharply than generations before them.

Somewhere between the generation of women raised in the forties and the generation of women who reached their years of adolescence and adulthood in the turbulent sixties, there arose this differentiation, this need to set one's own generation apart from the previous one. The women of the forties talk about differences in their era, compared to their parents generation, but they speak with pride of the closely knit, extended families and communities that enabled them to survive the tough times. In many ways, too, their experience of surviving has a sense of kinship and commonality with their parents and grandparents who were also survivors of immigration, famine, and the First

World War. One senses the continuity that binds them to the past. All that is broken sometime in the 1950s and 1960s. Although the significant events did not happen at the same time everywhere, the "generation gap" emerged.

The "age of the flower child" was what the women in PEI called the sixties. While I still have an easier time picturing flower children in Toronto's Yorkville district than amid the rolling brown hills of PEI, I think I know what they meant. These were the rebellious years of unrest and turbulence of a kind not previously known. "The late sixties was a very volatile time," was how another woman summed it up. I can't help but think this is something of an understatement.

The biggest marker of the sixties was, for most women, an event that happened in the United States. The assassination of President John Kennedy in 1963. "It was the end of an era. We had moved from the safety of the fifties into the sixties," they said. "Things were under control as long as JFK was alive. Even in Canada, the impact of his death was huge. The world as we knew it was ending."

How is it that an event in the US had such significance for Canadian women that not only do women recall what happened, they can also recall where they were and what they were doing when they first heard the news? It was perhaps something to do with the fragile shell that had been constructed in the post-war era. The apparent security and tranquility of those times was a thinner veneer than might be supposed. The war was only a few years in the past, the horrors scarcely dimmed from memory, and already there was the looming spectre of even greater devastation—the communist threat, real or perceived, and the very real dangers of the growing arsenal of nuclear weapons. The Cold War was not really very cool after all. The generation of parents who so longed to shelter their children from the horrors they had experienced were busy building bomb shelters, teaching their young to hide under their desks if they heard sirens, constructing a Distant Early Warning Line across the far north that might prevent bombs from reaching Washington with Canada as a buffer! The death of a US president was surely more than enough to shatter this fragile peace of mind. If Kennedy could die, anything was possible. The calm and apparent security of the fifties was only skin-deep. In an instant, it gave way to the upheaval of the sixties.

"It was a time of great uncertainty and, at the same time, great liberation." This generation shared with the women socialized in the fifties, an overriding positive outlook on themselves, the world, the future. "The Cold War was going on but there was a general sense of optimism," said one women. "There were problems, restrictions, big changes, but this was a time of liberation," said another.

"We believed 'we can do it differently.' We believed in the future." One women talked about the sixties as "the beginning of the social justice era." This kind of mindset it seemed to me, tended to distinguish the two subgroups of

Challengers. It wasn't just that the sixties generation believed in the future, in a positive sense, they were convinced they could change it. They were critically aware of the problems of the present, of issues from nuclear bombs to racism to pollution. And they firmly believed in their own power to change the future. It seems to me no coincidence that this was the decade in which Canada introduced universal access to health care, through the Canada Health Act, and many other facets of the social security net.

"This generation takes change well because it's always been part of life," said one woman. There is no question that there was a marked change between the attitudes of the Challengers and the Strivers. For many Challengers, change is associated with positive connotations—progress, social change, improvement in quality of life, changing the world, challenging the status quo. The vision and values may differ from person to person but there is a similarity in outlook on change as a whole. The striking characteristic of this generation, whether of the 1950s or the 1960s, is the belief in personal ability to make a difference. Shaped in an era of rapid, almost mind-boggling change, came a generation with enormous self-confidence, indeed with the belief that they had the power to change the world.

Calculators: Gone the Security of the Past

Walrath's final category, the Calculators, are those born after 1955, the women whose years of socialization took place largely in the seventies and early eighties. These are women who were under forty-five in 2000, born just at the end of or after the end of the baby boom. In the Naomi's Daughters workshops, as in our churches, there weren't very many of these women around.

There aren't as many of them demographically of course—the baby boom was just that, a big bulge in the population. As the baby boomers had children, they eventually produced a smaller little bump on the population curve, the so-called Echo that came later on. In the middle is this much smaller group. It is a group of women who all their lives have looked around and wondered, "where is everyone?" Of course, the church has also asked this group the same question. I remember as I entered Sunday school and youth groups being faced with that persistent, though sometimes unspoken question, "where has everyone gone?"

"We were always told about those enormous Sunday school classes and those wonderful big youth groups of the 1950s and 1960s. I remember feeling slightly guilty that there weren't more of us." Of course, demographics wasn't all there was to it, at least not in the church, but certainly we had the same experience elsewhere in society.

When asked about the pivotal experiences of their years of acculturation, those at the tail end or just off the end of the baby boom talked about their feeling of having missed out on something. "I grew up with this sense of having just missed the party," was how one woman described this.

This group of women entered adulthood not with a sense of limitless possibilities so characteristic of the sixties, but with a sense of closing down and of limitations. There were fewer places for students. There were tough times economically for many as well as big changes in rural areas from grain gluts and depressed prices to the rural depopulation that has continued to the present day.

Women of this age group talked about the nuclear threat and the environment as grave and pressing concerns. "The world was coming to be seen as fragile and limited," said one. The women went on to describe their growing awareness of the global impact of events.

The oil crisis was another key event of the seventies, another reminder of limits, of an end to the perception of limitless opportunity so predominant in the fifties and sixties. The formation of the Organization of Petroleum Exporting Countries (OPEC) for the first time brought together oil-producing nations, which had a dramatic impact on the price and availability of crude oil. In 1973, Arab oil producers raised crude oil prices by 70 percent, and cut production by 5 percent. One woman described the impact this way. "It was as though suddenly the powers that be realized that other countries might have power over North America!" High inflation, in part a result of the oil crisis eventually gave way to global recession, higher unemployment, and cutbacks in government spending. By the end of 1981, unemployment in Canada had created a group of jobless people larger than the ranks of the nation's armed services during the Second World War.

"The globe is smaller. Instant communication has changed our perceptions," was another comment on the times. This group reached adolescence watching the world's "first televised war," as nightly newscasts etched scenes of Vietnam—the My Lai Massacre, bombings, and napalm—into the memories of this generation of young adults. Famine was also on the TV screen, in particular the famine in Biafra (a region of eastern Nigeria whose unsuccessful secessionist movement, 1967–70, resulted in thousands of deaths in a war-induced famine).

The end of the Vietnam War in 1975 brought thousands of refugees, the so-called Vietnamese boat people, to Canadian shores and increased Canada's involvement in refugee aid. The generation socialized in the seventies and eighties was entering a world of instant communication and global news coverage that, if not always in-depth, was immediate. The world truly had grown smaller and the isolated bubble of the 1950s was only a distant memory.

Feminism was also a pivotal event for women in this age group. Although some still mourned the changing roles and, in particular, the ever-increasing divorce rate, most in this age group seemed to view the changes in women's rights and women's roles very positively. "There was that awful label 'women's libbers' but this was a time when feminism really came into its own in a positive way," said one woman. Women mentioned the United Nations decade for women, the more equal sharing of roles, and greater opportunities for women. "I moved into adulthood with more developed ideas about equality and rights. We read books by Canadian women. It was possible for women to be ministers." All sorts of new possibilities were opening up, it seemed. "Women have become a lot more independent in both the working world and home life. This has allowed women to openly express their views and hopes," said others.

Divorce, single parenting, remarrying, and blended families were all issues faced by this generation. Of course, none of these issues was new, but by the late 1970s the divorce rate in Canada was nearing 40 percent. "Opening doors for women," challenges to the "patriarchal male dominated 'way things are,'" "choices," " a new kind of questioning" are all phrases these women used to describe what was happening.

There was something else afoot, though, that brought out the more negative sense of the times. True, this was the decade that saw the end of the Vietnam War, but the end came with virtually none of the jubilation of 1945. The impeachment hearings of President Richard Nixon begun in May, 1974, and his resignation that August, a year and a half after the Paris Peace accord ended US involvement in Vietnam, suggested something quite different. Some women called it a "breakdown in authority structures." I think what they were referring to was the change in the "givens" brought about in large part by the boomer generation.

No longer did clergy, teachers, principals, parents, even presidents have a taken-for-granted authority. The threatened impeachment of a president, which many women mentioned, may have symbolized the dismantling of something far bigger—the whole fabric of the society was being called into question. The challenging of authority structures gave a whole new twist to the meaning of "generation gap." It was perhaps as though this generation no longer needed to state that they were different from their parents. It was so obvious that no one needed to even verbalize it.

Changes in sexuality and sexual behaviour that had began in the 1960s continued into this generation. "Sex, drugs, and rock 'n' roll," were replaced by sex, disco, and the new street drugs of the 1970s.

This generation's sense of itself was strikingly different from the women of the fifties and sixties. The Challengers' optimism about the future was completely reversed in a few short years. "Our generation was much more insecure, we had a lack of optimism about the future," was one woman's way of summing up this perception. Others talked about a pervading sense of disillusionment. "We were duped into believing that we could have it all, to enjoy life's banquet to the fullest, that we were entitled to a bountiful life. But we were confronted constantly by closed doors, limits—limited opportunities, limited resources."

Women of the Calculator's cohort knew that full employment and a secure future were things of the past. "There was a different sense of women's role. I felt that money and having a career were very important." Calculators really did have to calculate, to plan ahead, in a way that was not so apparent for a generation before. Within every generation there have been those on the margins, the poor and vulnerable within the society. But something happened in the 1970s or, more likely a whole cluster of things actually, to change a whole generation's perception of the future. The optimistic "we can change the world" vision of the 1960s, or "the future will be fine" of the 1950s came to be replaced by a more pessimistic view of life. The world was limited, the power of people to change was limited, and you had to be tough to survive.

It wasn't just that the seventies cohort felt they had to work hard to get ahead, sometimes they felt they had to work hard to stay in the same place. Words like "stress" and "burnout" entered the vocabulary. Changing roles for women were not always so very liberating. Many women simply picked up an extra load, the so-called "double day" of work, child care, and housework.

"There is a belief not only that we can do everything but that we *should* do everything," this group said, as they talked about this myth of the "superwoman." "My generation has a busy stressful time to cope with all the juggling we have to do, time, work, finances. The older generation lived through hard times but sometimes I think, compared to the race we live in today, those were good times." There's no question that the expansive open horizons of a previous decade had been replaced by a sense of burden, anxiety, and stress.

It is harder to judge the full impact on this generation of these stresses and changes, because, in a sense, we are still seeing that generation unfold into mature adulthood. The women said of themselves that they are more cautious, more wary of the future. And right now what they most want other women to know about their lives is how stressed and overworked they feel, that they have a chronic shortage of time, that they're doing best that they can, and that much of the time life feels like being in a pressure cooker.

The Echo Generation: The End of Security

And what of the generation now in their teens and twenties? This was by far the smallest group in the workshops, and of course it is impossible to judge how the years in which they are being acculturated will affect them. Like the generations of women socialized in the sixties and later, they are keenly aware of generational differences, however. When asked how they think their generation's experience may be different from previous generations, technology is high on the list.

The advent of the microchip has brought vast changes, particularly computer-based technology. They are keenly aware of how quickly technology is changing—they know because of the computer programs they use, and the systems they have to use them. This age group is using technology that did not exist ten or even five years ago, and using it with fluency and ease. It seems as though e-mail, faxes, and CDs have always been here. Many of this age group used computers before they learned to read. They really *do* know the difference between a hard drive and a floppy, between megabytes and gigabytes. They set up their own web pages, program their parents' VCRs, carry pagers or cell phones, and browse the World Wide Web. One young teen said jokingly, "Between internet, TV, and computer games we have twice as much stuff to replace our families as our parents did when they were teenagers!"

Joking aside, growing up in the eighties and nineties hasn't been easy for them. "Maybe we never lived through a war or Depression, but growing up was still hard, we weren't all spoiled. Drugs and violence were large threats when we growing up," they say.

Other differences they noted included AIDS, of course. In this generation AIDS has always been there. It was there in the background as they reached sexual maturity; it is always a factor when they think about relationships. It didn't yet exist when most of their parents were teenagers, and certainly hadn't reached public consciousness until a decade and a half ago, but it has changed the way a whole generation thinks about sexuality and relationships.

"The way we view relationships is different in other ways too," say these young women. "The people we marry or go out with could be from anywhere, literally anywhere in the world. Our world is so small." This came from young women in rural PEI. Unlike their parents, their world is more diverse, more multicultural. And the older they get the more diverse it seems, particularly on university campuses or as they move into urban areas for work or education. But even in the rural community, their sense of the world is both more interconnected with other places and cultures and more diverse.

The awareness of same-gender couples is another issue they raise. Of course there is still homophobia, they acknowledge. "Our generation is a lot less judgmental about that lifestyle. We're much more open-minded and accepting of different kinds of choices. I think our society is more accepting. There are more options. Boundaries are less clear." I have heard this from other youth. Young people do tend to think in less rigid categories about sexuality. Even their notion of sexual orientation seems less rigid, less "either/ or," more fluid. Sexuality is viewed more in terms of choices one makes than as something predetermined by cultural norms, expectations, or biology.

Much in their world is more fluid, less predictable, more open-ended than that of previous generations. They had this to say about the future: "We have to go to college and university or we know we're not going to have jobs. It is going to take us a lot longer to get educated." The enormous advances in technology mean you need more schooling, they think, but also they expect that they will probably need at least two degrees or very specialized training if they want to find a place for themselves in the new economy.

The issue of women working outside the home isn't one they raise at all. If they aren't already working, they are certainly hoping or planning to do so in the future, and even the younger teens are starting to think about what they're going to do. The 1980s brought an incredible reduction in job security. Home-based work replaced office work; contract jobs and layoffs replaced permanent work. The commitment of the workplace to the worker has eroded in favour of the bottom line. Many young people are very pessimistic about the prospects of finding stable employment. And they know they can expect to have not just one career but several different ones over the course of their working life. It is easy to feel discouraged, they say, pointing out that some young people really are giving up. If you don't think you have what it takes to survive in this tough and competitive, information driven environment, it's easy to give up hope.

As a group, they aren't very optimistic about the future of the planet. Things like the environment, global climate change, the economy, the changing nature of work, weigh heavily on their minds.

Janet O'Neill

The early spring sun felt good on the back of her neck. Janet rested her head on her hands. In the background she could hear the cheers of the parents, "Go Mike!" "Good play, Samantha." The chocolate bar sales were going okay; there would be more than enough to cover the field rental and uniforms. She looked up in time to catch a glimpse of Meagan in full flight down the field, after the ball. "Meagan, get back here!" she yelled, abandoning the chocolate bars to race after her.

Tucking the squalling Meagan under one arm she trudged back up the field. "She's just about fried," she said to one of the other soccer mums above Meagan's yells. "Mind if I just give her a break. Can you watch the snacks? I'll be back in twenty."

She hauled Meagan into the car and wordlessly drove across the street to the mall. She could pick up some cans for the food drive at Blaise's after-four and get the Sunday school juice at the same time; she'd forgotten to do it yesterday after work. Meagan would holler her lungs out, but at least the supermarket had Meagan-proof safety straps on the carts.

By the time she got back to the soccer field Meagan's screeches had dulled to faint sobs, but Blaise was in a full-fledged tantrum. One of the dads was trying to calm him down, but not having much luck. "Blaise kind of lost it when he missed a goal," one of the mums said gently. She was trying to sound sympathetic, but Janet was in no mood for sympathy. She grabbed Blaise by the arm and fled the field. She didn't want all the perfect parents to see her tears.

In church the next morning, she sat at the back behind Jodi and Clare. She had learned to choose her seats with care. Jodi and Clare wouldn't give her "the look" if the kids squirmed, which, at this moment, they most definitely were. "Will you sit still," she hissed to Blaise, praying silently for the prayer to be over. And if you act up in Sunday school today, I'm..." her voice trailed off because she wasn't sure what she would do if the Sunday school teachers came to get her again. She prayed silently that Blaise would be good enough, or Clare patient enough, to give her the thirty minutes of peace she so desperately needed.

The teachers didn't come to get her. All through the sermon, silent tears streamed down her face. She did pray, for strength, for some kind of wisdom she didn't feel she had, for whatever it was that would get her through. During the announcements she heard Peggy Foster's appeal for help with the pie distribution and something about the kitchen, but she wasn't really listening. All she really wanted to do was just sit there, just sit.

Peggy Foster

Peggy Foster picked a crushed flower off one of the Easter lilies. Some of the lilies had been damaged when the children stomped past them on Sunday. Meagan O'Neill had been personally responsible for crushing at least two fine white trumpets.

Martha's Circle was going to deliver the lilies to shut-ins, which really meant Betty, Mary, Mavis, and herself would be delivering. The others didn't drive anymore. Well, Thelma still drove but Thelma behind a wheel wasn't something anyone really liked to encourage. There were fifty-two shut-ins on the list, so that's thirteen apiece, she calculated. Mavis could take the ones up to Central Lodge; that was near her home. Peggy continued tidying up the lilies. Delivering the lilies was one of the jobs she actually liked, especially the look on the elderly faces when she arrived with a bright, white potted lily. She liked to stop and chat for a bit, knowing how lonely these women were.

Mrs. Cartmen always told stories of the Challenge Unit, and the old days of the Woman's Missionary Society and Woman's Association, when there were several groups all meeting regularly. Mrs. Cartmen really missed the contact, she said, but these days it's just so hard to get out. You know how it is.

Peggy Foster did know. Certainly she knew a lot about loneliness, especially since Charlie's death; not being able to get out was one of her biggest fears. Her arthritis was acting up more and more and she really didn't know how much longer she'd be able to keep this all going. What do you do when you can't get out? How do you keep connected to the rest of the world, or do you watch it simply move on without you?

It was a bit of a rush to get all the lilies done in one day, and lilies don't really keep all that well, not after being in church and getting moved around and all the temperature changes. They really could use about five more people on the route. "But I'm not going to get up there and make another plea for help and have no one but Thelma offer to do a thing," she vowed. "Thelma has done her time!"

Peggy had one more lily left over at the end of her rounds. She debated leaving it at the church for Rev. Berkley, but to tell the truth, the Reverend was not very good with lilies, didn't water them. In the end she decided to deliver it to Janet O'Neill. The poor thing really had looked very teary on Sunday. Janet was out, but she left a note wishing Janet a happy Easter. It was just as well she didn't stop in, she thought. She'd have enough time to deliver the empty margarine containers to the foodbank before it closed.

Jodi Morrison

Jodi eyed the clock anxiously. Seven-thirty and still no sign of Rebekah.

"You're sure Becky didn't call?" she called upstairs to Gin.

"I already told you that a zillion times, Mum, she didn't call, and she's not with Brenda because I just talked to her sister." Gin sounded peeved, but underneath her annoyance Jodi knew she too was worried.

The phone rang. Jodi picked it up on the first ring. It wasn't Rebekah, only Mrs. Newberry from church.

"Hi Jodi," Mrs. Newberry began cheerily. "I'm just calling you to about a little gathering I'm organizing about the plans the CD committee is making, you know the restructuring…"

"Yes?" said Jodi politely, knowing full well what was coming next.

"Well, we're having a little meeting next Thursday and we'd really like some input from parents of teens, you know, the older children's perspective…"

Jodi hesitated. "Thursday? Let me see…well, that's the day I usually drive the girls to their practice, and…"

Mrs. Newberry sighed. It was only a little sigh, but Jodi heard it. "She's wondering what's wrong with the buses, or why teens these days are so spoiled they have to get driven everywhere," thought Jodi.

"It's just that, well, I like to keep an eye on them," she tried to answer the unspoken question. "And the buses don't run all that regularly at night." Really, it was to make sure Rebekah actually got there and didn't just spend the evening hanging out with who knows whom. And to have a moment of contact that wasn't an argument. Sometimes, slouched out of sight behind her in back seat, Rebekah would actually say something.

"It's all right. You're very busy, I understand," said Mrs. Newberry. Jodi could tell that she didn't.

"I'm sorry…" said Jodi lamely.

"Oh, that's quite alright," said Mrs. Newberry briskly.

Angie Henders

Angie glanced up at the library clock. Six-thirty. She logged off and began stuffing her various folders of notes into her pack. She hadn't got very far and mid-terms were looming dangerously close, but she agreed to meet up with Clarence and Tom for supper. They were waiting outside the library, when she came running down the steps.

"About time you got here," said Tom, pretending to pout.

"Where are we going for supper?" she asked.

"Michelangelo's," said Clarence extravagantly. "Pizza on the house, our treat!"

Over supper they talked about the chem. lab, their homework in general, and the demonstration against fee hikes.

"I figure I'm already going to be spending the rest of my working life paying off student loans," Clarence moaned.

"That's assuming you even get a job," said Tom.

"And that there even is a future to spend our working lives in," said Angie. She laughed. She was starting to sound as pessimistic as the church youth group.

"Hey, I almost forgot, we're going mountain biking tomorrow," said Clarence. "Tom's sister is driving us up to Mt. Ste. Marie. Want to come?"

"I can't," said Angie.

"Oh come on, take a break for a day. The library isn't even open on Sunday morning."

"No, it's just that I've got this group I lead."

"Oh yeah, I keep forgetting. Your *religious* obligations!"

"I have the hardest time picturing you in a Sunday dress and hat," teased Tom.

"Funny, I can't picture you in one either," she countered.

"I can!" laughed Clarence.

"Oh shut up. You know I don't even *own* a decent dress." Tom was getting into this now.

"What is it you do, exactly?" Clarence was more serious. "I mean, why do you go to church?"

Angie didn't know quite how to explain. "I don't know. I like the kids in the youth group I guess. People are nice. I can get away from you two idiots for a while…"

7

Frameworks in the Church

The earth shattering changes of the last five decades have left their mark on the church as on every other facet of Canadian society. Not only has the church changed over time, each generation of women entering the church has brought its particular generational perspective into the church. How do generational differences influence the ways women view the church? How do they affect what we offer to or expect of the church? How do our differences affect the way we interact with one another, the activities we choose to get involved in, or how we participate in the church?

What Generational Differences Can Predict

Before we can address these questions, however, we need to go back once more to the issue of what generational differences can and cannot predict. Individual women are very different from one another. Knowing the age of a women will not tell us what she thinks, believes, or values, nor can it predict the choices an individual woman may make or the ways she interacts with the church or with other women. Individual women may differ significantly from the general "culture" of their generation.

Although it may be true that most women in a particular generation will hold the framework of that generation, certainly some will not. As noted earlier, once a generational framework evolves, it becomes available and is sometimes adopted by women of other generations. Different frameworks might characterize each generation in very general terms or broad strokes, but they will never fully describe individual women. What is most important, ultimately, is that we begin to understand that these kinds of differences exist, not that we try to slot women of any particular age groups into rigid categories. While it may be true that most women of a particular age group identify with the framework of that generation, when I write about any given generation's framework, I am really writing about those who identify with that framework, whatever their age.

Understanding the unique "culture" or framework of different generations may help us understand ourselves and others, but it cannot be used to pigeonhole. As a tool to understand general trends or patterns, it may be helpful. As a way to predict, prescribe, or stereotype, it may block and inhibit trust and understanding.

Having said that, it is still possible to note some general trends within each generation of women in the church, and those who identify with that generational framework, as a way of understanding and appreciating how our differences affect us as women in the church.

Strivers in the Church

The Striver generation, as identified earlier, are those women who are now in their late sixties and older. For women who identify with the Striver generation, a sense of duty, obligation, and responsibility predominate. These were the values of their time, values that helped their generation endure. In the struggle to survive the crises of war and Depression, this generation developed a strong work ethic and a strong sense of "hanging together" as a community. These same kinds of values—hard work, persistence, hanging in, holding the group together—are characteristic of their church involvement.

In the era in which this group reached adulthood, the church was at the centre of community and social life. The authority of the minister was a given, the authority of the church was a given, and for the most part God was taken for granted, just as the existence of the church and one's participation in it was assumed. There were exceptions, to be sure, but this was the predominant view.

This is a generation that grew up with stability as the norm, and change as the aberration. Therefore, this tends to be a generation that expects the church to be there, unchanging and forever. These women also assume that they will be there, as long as they are able, to support and maintain the church. Words like "loyal" and "steadfast" describe their attitude to the church. They are deeply committed and give high priority to living out their responsibility to support the church.

Most of the women in the Striver cohort grew up in churches with predominantly male leadership. Most would not have experienced women in ordained ministry; in those days most women ministers were deaconesses and, as one woman from this generation pointed out, "women were expected to play a supportive role. It really was socially difficult and not very acceptable for women to be [ordained] ministers." This may colour some women's perceptions of the role women should play in the church—in fact, many of this age group may consciously or unconsciously maintain that women should still be in supportive roles, adjunct to the male leadership of the church.

Raised in a time of highly structured social authority, which was reinforced by the war years, Strivers also bring a particular perspective to authority in the church. Often women in this age group maintain a high regard for the position of ordained clergy and expect their ministerial leaders to be role models and leaders in the church and wider community. Members of the Striver cohort may place high value on the traditions, beliefs, and teachings of the church. The "givens" of the teachings with which they were raised give many women of this generation a strong and steady faith perspective.

Challengers in the Church

The women who are now in their mid-forties to late sixties view the church very differently from the previous generation. For the most part they view participation in the church as a choice, not an obligation. Because they were socialized in a world where values and social norms were in such flux, as a group they tend to see issues of religion and morality in more relativistic terms. Clergy or the traditional teachings of the church often do not have the same kind of authority for them as for the Strivers. Challengers might have chosen the values or beliefs of the church, but they know there are other options available to them. Challengers are driven more by interests, ethics, and personal commitment than by a sense of socially imposed duty, "ought," or obligation.

This does not mean, of course, that those of the Challenger framework are any less committed to the church. Their commitment and loyalty may be very strong indeed, but it arises from a different source. Larger society has not imbued those of the Challenger generation and younger with the same sense of obligation about the church. If they are involved in a significant way, it is because they see a larger value and purpose to such involvement. If they come to church, it is because they choose to do so.

Socialized in an era of rapid social upheaval, in which the big baby-boom cohort brought about such significant social change, Challengers often perceive themselves as change-makers or as capable of bringing about significant change. They also tend to view change much more positively than the generation before them. Very often Challengers see the church as a place to act on their beliefs, to make a difference in the church or in the world around such issues as racism, gender-equality, militarism, and global justice. Again, this is not to say that other age groups do not hold these same kinds of commitments. But the Challenger cohort are more likely to see things like "making a difference" or "bringing about change" as a primary reason to be involved in the church.

Change is quite normal for the Challenger generation. They are not surprised by changes in the church; in fact they are often very interested in creating change. The Challenger cohort breezed through the church in a time of great expansion. The 1960s was a time of church building—new churches in the suburbs and new Christian education wings on older churches to accommodate the expanding numbers of boomers and their families. Challengers picked up the optimism of the times, and the "get involved and make a difference" mentality. They may not operate out of the same kind of sense of duty as the Strivers, but they will certainly get behind efforts they support in the interests of making a difference in the church and in the larger society. This, after all, is the generation that grew up believing that it could indeed change the world.

During the era in which this Challenger cohort reached adulthood, the church itself was embroiled in change, much like the society around it. One woman in the Naomi's Daughters workshops jokingly pointed to one of the "big changes" in the church in the mid-sixties—the wearing of hats in church became optional for women! We laughed about the hats but, even as we laughed, we knew the hats pointed to something deeper. Hats for women in church had once been a social convention, harkening back to the words of Paul in his letter to the Corinthians that women should keep their heads covered in church as a sign that they were under the authority of their husbands (1 Cor. 11:10). Christ, husband, wife—that was once the order, the structure of social authority. Then came the Challenger generation and society was turned on its head. And a small but significant sign of these changing times was that women no longer wore hats in church.

The changing roles for women in society began to be felt in the church. Women became more prominent in leadership—on boards and committees and also, although this was still rare, in ordained leadership. In the era of the Woman's Missionary Society and Woman's Association and the early days of the UCW, women were not fully integrated into the power and decision-making structures of the church. Some congregations simply did not elect women as elders or stewards, although there was no official policy against this. Women's power and leadership were exercised largely within the women's organizations. As women of the Challenger's cohort pointed out, all that changed along with the hats.

Some women of this age-group even went so far as to suggest that perhaps women no longer needed the traditional women's organizations as places to live out their ministry, because they could now do so fully within the larger church structures. In any case, it is certainly true that the Challenger cohort has had much greater access to and involvement in the decision-making bodies of the church, and certainly was socialized in an era that increasingly expected that to be the case.

The other big change of the Challenger generation, at least in the United Church, was the introduction of the New Curriculum. This was a curriculum written just around the time that the hordes of baby-boom children came flooding into United Church Sunday schools. In many ways it was a curriculum designed for the baby boomers, very much in tune with the times. Introduced in 1964, around the same time that the hats disappeared, the New Curriculum brought a totally new approach to scripture and Christian education. Gone were the catechisms of the past, to be replaced by a critical study of scripture using contemporary scholarship.

The new curriculum replaced a notion of authoritative church teaching with study that allowed for other interpretations. True to its time, a single voice of "correct doctrine" or "the" answers to questions of faith was replaced by open-ended exploration of Bible stories and faith in general. Some viewed this as "the beginning of the end" while others welcomed the new approach as a breath of fresh air. The new curriculum was a sign of its times, turning upside down or inside out the predictable social order of the past, including how the Bible was to be studied and taught.

The social upheaval and questioning in which the Challenger generation reached adulthood brought questions, critical thinking, and the possibility for diversity of opinion into the church. This is not to say that the only critical and challenging thinkers in the church are the people under sixty-eight and, of course, diversity of opinion in the church had existed long before the Challengers ever came along. However, critique and a new kind of individualism are very characteristic of the Challenger group. To claim something as true simply on the basis of the traditional teaching of the church has little currency with this cohort.

The Challenger generation, and all subsequent ones, expect to find and discern faith for themselves. Any sense of an absolute and objective truth is vastly diminished if not vanished altogether. "The truth" was replaced by diverse interpretations and beliefs. Truth and morality once were understood as objective "fact"; now they are up for discussion.

For the Striver generation, belonging to the church was a given, because that was what one was "supposed" to do. Belief flowed automatically from the simple act of belonging. "If you belonged to the church you simply believed most of what the church believed," said one woman of the Striver age group. "You weren't really expected to question it. If you weren't sure about something you more or less took it on faith because that's what the church said about it." Challengers don't usually believe because that's what the church has told them to believe. Many of them simply can't suspend their capacity for critical questioning and doubt that was so much a part of their formative years. This doesn't mean that the Challengers have faith that is less deep than those of the Striver era. It does mean that they expect to struggle more with their faith, and perhaps that they take it less for granted.

We no longer live in an era when the church has all the answers, or in which we can depend on the authority of a church leader to figure out the answers to the tough questions and tell us what to do. We live in a world of many different faiths and many different belief systems, within a society that tends to say that what an individual wants to believe is largely up to that individual. Challengers bring their questions into the church, but they don't expect the church to tell them the final answers and most especially, they don't want the church to tell them what to do.

Calculators in the Church

Calculators, those women who are now between twenty and forty-five, have yet a different involvement in and relationship to the church. Calculators were socialized in the post-boom era of cutbacks and recession. Their view of the world was shaped by a sense of limits, environmental crisis, impermanence, and uncertainty. Not surprisingly the stresses of living in such a context of insecurity has influenced what they expect and need from the church. Calculators, more than any other previous generation, view the church as a place of support and in some instance even as a refuge from the world around them. Many of them expect the church to support and nurture them spiritually.

Unlike the Challengers, who expect to make a difference when they get involved in the church, or the Strivers, who see it as an obligation to support the church, the Calculators are often looking to the church as a place where they, and their children, can find spiritual or emotional support they need to help them cope with the demands of daily life.

Calculators are acutely aware that there are limits to the world's resources. This sense of limits affects their own awareness of their own limited resources of time, energy, and money. They expect to make choices; if they are involved in the church (and many of their peers are not) they expect the church to be worth the effort—in other words, they expect the church to address their interests and needs. If not, they may look elsewhere—for another church, another social or community setting, or another way of addressing their spiritual needs.

Calculators live in a world that seems to them limited and insecure. They feel the stresses and tensions of modern life most acutely, and often describe themselves as being "pulled in many directions." One woman summed it up this way, "I have full-time work, and kids that feel like full-time work on top of that. I simply can't squeeze another thing in! I feel stretched to the limit, sometimes even beyond the limit." What she needs, she says, is something that takes the pressure off, not something that adds more work.

She has found that in a group that meets for spirituality and faith reflection. This group of women, who are mostly in their forties and fifties, never use the church kitchen. "We bring our own coffee, in thermoses or carry-out mugs." In fact, there was a major conflict at one point about the cleaning of the kitchen. The existing women's groups rotated responsibility for oversight and cleaning of the kitchen, but the spirituality group objected, "We never use it, so we don't see why we should have to clean it. There was a big split over that."

Obviously this isn't just about cleaning or kitchens. It's about perceptions, choices, sense of responsibility, sense of ownership, roles. The spirituality group doesn't see the kitchen as their responsibility. It's not a duty they feel they owe the church. After all, church itself isn't a duty, so why should they feel obligated to take care of the kitchen. Furthermore, their awareness of women's changing roles means they don't so readily accept women's traditional caretaking responsibility.

For many older women there is a sense of duty or obligation about attending church and supporting the women's organizations. Helping the church, whether by raising funds, cleaning the kitchen, or some other form of service, is something one really *should* do. For younger women, church involvement is a choice, one option they may have chosen from a variety of other possibilities. For them, involvement in church is not something they have to do, but something they have chosen because it meets their needs, provides an outlet for them to live out their values, helps them develop and express their spirituality, and provides a community. But, if church didn't meet these needs, they would look elsewhere. The corollary of this is that they might *choose* to bake for the UCW tea, but they don't *have* to.

The Echo Generation in the Church

The youngest women who attended the Naomi's Daughters workshops were women in their teens and early twenties. Not only is church attendance no longer an expectation or a duty, it makes them something of an oddity in their peer group. Those who came to the workshops have obviously chosen to maintain a connection to the church, but this is a choice that goes very much against the prevailing current of their generation. Church participation is often considered very "un-cool" and peers raise their eyebrows more than a bit if they know you go to church.

"Most of our friends aren't here," they say, "so the church cannot possibly be the centre of our social life the way it was for our mothers or grandmothers. If we just hung out there, we'd never see any of our friends!" They want to be with their peer group, and some do indeed find small groups of like-minded peers in the church. But church is only one part of their lives, often a very small part, competing with other interests and demands on their time—work, sports, school, other social commitments or volunteer work, and friendships outside the church.

There is a tendency to view this youngest age group as "non-believers." It is true that many of them have not been raised in the church and, even if they were, they may not choose the church of their parents. However, research shows that teens do have strong beliefs—in God, in the value of prayer, even in such things as the divinity of Jesus. According to the research of Canadian sociologist Reginald Bibby (Bibby 1990, 86) the percentage of teens and adults who believe in these things varies very little. The big differences occur when it comes to matters of organizational participation or church attendance. A recent Angus Reid survey found that 31 percent of those fifty-five and older attended church weekly, while only 15 percent of those eighteen to thirty-four do (*Globe and Mail*, 22 April 2000, A1, A10).

Young women often have big questions about life and about spiritual matters. They may be looking to the church as a place to share some of their questions and their spiritual longing, but they may also bring with them some degree of suspicion and mistrust. They don't want to be told what to do, or what to believe, but are looking for a safe space in which to explore, a place that can allow them to "be themselves." Their disinterest or suspicion of institutions and organized structures extends to organized religion. Faith itself has become highly privatized and less tied to institutional participation.

Youth often feel quite marginalized within the church. Not only do they find themselves in a significant minority (about 60 percent of regular church goers are over sixty) (Bibby 1994), they sometimes find themselves if not alienated, at least significantly misunderstood. As one young woman described it, "the church doesn't give enough time to listening to younger voices."

Separate Groups

Given these vast differences in framework and experience, it is not surprising that women in our churches have tended to form separate groups. To some extent, the women in the Naomi's Daughters workshops felt it was only natural that women congregate in their own age groupings. Friendships and interests do tend to form within age groups.

Things like time and schedules and the different interests of different age groups were identified. Older and younger women have definite preferences about *when* to meet, for example. Older women prefer afternoon meetings and find evenings harder. Health, safety, and fatigue all make it a less preferable option. Younger women usually work outside the home, usually during the daytime. Evening meetings are the only possibility for most of them.

Even many of the existing UCW groups have several "units" within a congregation that may be loosely divided along age lines. But that has always been the case and does not fully explain the sense of distance or lack of mutual understanding that women feel, nor the present crisis in women's organizations. Why didn't new groups of younger women simply join in on the tail end of the existing UCW, as happened in the past?

The UCW is clearly patterned on a framework of the Striver generation—its hallmarks are hard work, long-term commitment, permanent membership, loyalty, dedication, service, and obligation. These are not attributes that draw in women of the Challenger age and younger. As one woman pointed out in reference to the idea that one should be part of a UCW group, "The idea that 'you do this because you should' is a generational response of women older than I am. That kind of thinking is Greek to women my age and younger."

Younger women also strongly resist the stereotypical definitions of "women's groups" and "women's work" in the church. Whether it's an accurate portrayal or not, the UCW has come to be associated with a more traditional understanding of women's role and responsibility. One woman in her early twenties struggled to describe how she felt. "I feel a resistance to being part of something that is stereotypically 'the women's group.' I want to move beyond stereotypes. It has something to do with identity—kind of like saying this isn't who I am." "If our group had been called 'UCW' I would never have joined," said one woman bluntly.

There really are at least four separate and distinct cohorts of women within our churches: those who identify with the Striver age group and see church as a duty and a responsibility; those who identify more with the Challenger cohort and want the church to support their interests and causes; those of the Calculator cohort who seek from the church support in their quest for meaning, spirituality, and community; and youth who often feel like outsiders within the church. No wonder women in our churches have divided into groups, very often by age. No wonder the younger women's groups meet for short studies or gather around particular foci and call themselves names like "Sophia's Circle" or "the women's Spirituality group" or "Roots and Wings"— words that evoke a spiritual quest—while older groups call themselves names like "Martha's circle" or the "Challenge Unit" and make one another honorary life members. However, the existence of separate and distinct groups of women has not eased the tensions, in some congregations it may even exacerbate them.

Born in ...	Formative years	Issues in the church	World view
1910–1924 **Strivers**	1930s	response to poor and needy, church seen as an obligation, centre of all life	· change is negative · value hard work, survival · need to conserve in order protect community and family
1920–1934 **Strivers**	1940s	refugees, anti-Semitism, Japanese internment	· change is negative · hard work, survival · community and family are important
1930–1944 **Strivers/ Early Challengers**	1950s	mission in the world, church still seen as central to community life	· things can "return to normal" · progress is positive · value security and stability · growing affluence and consumerism
1940–1954 **Challengers**	1960s	civil rights, apartheid, racism, disarmament, church growth	· social change, we can make a difference · change is possible, and positive
1950–1964 **Calculators**	1970s	apartheid, human rights, refugees, church less central, viewed as a choice	· change is possible, and positive · but there is a growing sense of limits to resources
1960–1974 **Calculators/ Early Echo Generation**	1980s	gender justice, sexuality, economic justice, refugees, human rights, membership decline	· limited resources, world is finite · future looks limited, scary · plan ahead to survive
1970–1984 **Echo Generation**	1990s	economy, environment, genetic engineering, aboriginal justice, society views church as peripheral	· change is rapid and pervasive · you have to "keep up" to survive · future looks bleak

8

Bringing Our Differences to Church

The Church Moves from Centre Stage

In the era when the Striver generation reached adulthood, the church was the centre of community and social life. The church was involved with virtually every facet of life. Indeed, community life itself was much more integrated. People knew one another because by and large people stayed within the community. The bank manager knew the storeowner who knew the farmer. And all of them knew and were known by the clergy.

In the Canada of the 1930s, 1940s, and, in some places, well into the 1950s, most people lived and worked and socialized and relaxed and went to school and church within the same community. Douglas Walrath points out that in this old style of community the church really was involved in all of life, but now, "a generation has grown up, most of whom have never experienced the church as present to all of life. To see the church and God in such a way is not only difficult for them; for many it also seems absurd" (Walrath 1987, 14). This is true for many of the Challengers. For the Calculators and women now in teens and twenties such integration of church and community life is even more remote.

Nowadays work, home, marketplace, and school are usually separated by geography. Industrialization of our society has created greater and greater compartmentalization and specialization, separating work from community from family from faith community from social or recreational areas. Institutions are increasingly specialized to deal with different facets of human need, challenging the traditional role of religion to deal with all dimensions of life. People shop, play sports, meet health care needs, get support dealing with emotional problems, work, do volunteer work, and attend church (if they do) in quite separate and isolated spheres. What is more, people of the Calculator generation and younger do not even *expect* these areas of life to be integrated. This difference becomes most apparent when one looks at women's involvement in the church.

Older women typically expect the church to be integrated into every facet of their life. The church meets a variety of different needs and they view their involvement in church as a "whole package" that might include recreation, family life, volunteer commitments, friendships, or social and community service. One older woman described the integration of church and life in this way. "My whole social life revolved around the small country church in our village. My parents were very much involved. Mother played the organ and directed the choir. My father was caretaker and Sunday school superintendent. My uncle was treasurer. My grandmother taught Sunday school."

A younger woman coming to church may look to the church to meet one or even a few of her needs but she hardly expects the institution to be at the centre of her life in the larger community. Her extended family may live miles away. She doesn't expect her minister to know the principal of her or her children's school, or her boss at work, or her next-door neighbour. *She* may not even know her next-door neighbour! She doesn't necessary anticipate that church will form the centre of her social circle. Although she may have close friends there, she also has friends with no church involvement. She may have many other volunteer commitments outside the church and may expect only an occasional volunteer involvement with church. With so many outside and fragmented parts of her life, she often describes the "juggling" that she has to do to hold it all together. She may very much resent what she perceives as extra "demands" from the church to take on more tasks or get involved in yet another activity.

Women of the Calculator age group often talk about how difficult it can be to cope with their fragmented and compartmentalized lives. They look to the church to help them cope with the stresses of work without job security, with the demands of single parenting, or with the anxiety they feel about the future.

They may attend church only infrequently, focusing primarily on work or family life, or they may become heavily involved in church but have little involvement in their local community, or they may simply try to "retreat" as much as possible from additional demands or expectations. No longer can it be assumed that they will be involved with the church, as a matter of course, nor that the church will have impact and influence in most other areas of their life.

The longing for integration may still exists—the longing to have the different parts of our lives connect and interrelate, rather than having to relate to so many different and largely unconnected groups and organizations. The reality, however, is that most women of my age know such integration happens rarely, if ever.

The shift of the church away from centre stage has been accompanied, not surprisingly, by a strong decline in church attendance over the decades. According to the research of Reginald Bibby, in the late 1940s around 50% of Protestants maintained they were weekly church goers, with the figure still close to 40% at the end of the 1950s. Now, barely over 20% report that kind of involvement. (Bibby 1993, 4) As the church has moved from an "ought" to a choice, many people have simply opted not to be involved. According to Bibby, Canadians still have deep spiritual needs, and strong beliefs, but they do not necessarily have an institutional commitment.

As United Church theologian Douglas Hall describes this reality, "We can no longer count on our congregations automatically renewing themselves, with generation after generation filing obediently into the pews vacated by their forebears. The days of automatic Christianity are over." (Jan. 2000, 22). When the Strivers reached adulthood the church was still part of the social establishment and could more or less take for granted its power, its status, and its future. By the time the Calculators arrived on the adult scene, church was on the periphery of society, and fewer and fewer of their peers had any church connection at all.

Generations and Giving

The differences and tensions between women are compounded by the very real problems many churches are facing due to their declining or aging membership. This increases the pressure on older members, who may be continuing to bear an heavier and heavier share of the workload, and in turn can lead to feelings of fear that no one will pick this up when they're not able to carry on or resentment because younger folk don't seem to be stepping into the breach. "Where are they?" they ask, in tones that make me think of "back of the neck" Orpah who turned her back on Naomi in her time of need. Issues of volunteering and financial donations—what we give and how we give it—can become big sources of tension. Younger women sometimes feel misunderstood or pressured. Older women may feel as though they are the only ones doing all the work or carrying the entire burden.

There is a perception in the church that younger women do not donate as much, either time or money, as older generations. While that is true on average *within* the church, it is not true in terms of overall patterns of giving. Young women may be volunteering their time and giving money, but often their involvement may be split among a variety of activities and institutions.

According to the 1994 *Unitrends* survey, both men and women over fifty-five give larger amounts of money to the church and give more regularly than younger adults. However, the key phrase here is *within the church*. The older members of our society are not necessarily the biggest givers to all charities. Judith Nichols, a demographic annalist in the United States, noted that men and women over sixty-five comprise 25% of the population but only 16% of all donors. Baby boomers make up 42% of the population but 47% of donors (Muir 1998).

Not surprisingly, the way in which people do their giving also varies with age. Older donors tend to give more through long-term pledges. They respond to appeals for "commitment" and "challenge" and are often motivated by a sense of obligation or faithfulness in their patterns of giving. Younger donors give to projects and short-term appeals and are motivated more by compassion, a sense of community, or concern about a particular issue. Within the church, older people are more likely to have a pattern of tithing or regular giving. Younger people may give more to particular programs or appeals, and more to organizations and causes outside the church.

Generations and Volunteerism

As for the issue of whether younger people volunteer their time, a 1998 study of volunteerism in Canada by Statistics Canada entitled *Caring Canadians, Involved Canadians* found that the rate of volunteerism among young people aged fifteen to twenty-four has doubled in the last ten years. The Statistics Canada data indicates that volunteer involvement tends to peak in middle age, when people have children involved in a number of activities that require volunteer help, and shows that 65 percent of volunteers are employed (*Globe and Mail* 25 Aug. 1998, A1, A6).

There are age differences in how people donate time, too. Younger volunteers (those of the Challenger age group and younger) are not as interested in making long-term commitments. The days of elders or Sunday school teachers or Stewards who were virtually appointed for life are long gone. Younger volunteers want to be involved on short-term projects, not committees. They want to get the job done, and they don't particularly like going to meetings.

Younger women clearly put in plenty of volunteer hours, not all of them in the church of course. In the workshops they often said that felt pulled in many different directions by the demands of home, work, community; their children's schools, clubs or sports activities. The statistics confirm what they say.

Some women of the Challenger cohort may resent the competing demands on the younger women's time or their apparent lack of interest in doing what needs to be done in and around the church. They may feel they are left to shoulder the whole burden. They complain about the lack of proper priorities. "Younger women just don't have time for church. They're too busy supporting their children's sports activities," they say. The women of older generations say, and rightly so, that they too were busy when they were young. Life wasn't easy during the hard years of war and Depression, and yet they still found time to support they church.

Younger women in turn may feel that every time they turn around someone in the church is asking or expecting them to do something. They may resent the added pressure on lives that often feel very pressured. "What I really want older women to know is how stressed I feel, and how many different things I am expected to do. Sometimes I feel like a wishbone, except that I'm not just pulled in two directions, it's more like six or seven," they say. Others make the claim that "women really do have less time. I am so pressured I simply couldn't squeeze another thing in." These statements are borne out by larger surveys. In a 1990 national survey Reginald Bibby found that time was a enormous issue for most Canadians, but pressure on time was most acute for women aged thirty-five to forty-four (Bibby 1993, 141). Women in this age group seemed to be at the extreme end of what is a typically Canadian problem to start with—lack of time!

For many older women the question, spoken or unspoken, is "what are these younger women doing with their time?" And when the latter answer "working," this poses another question for older generations. "Do they really need to be working full time, since we learned to make do with a lot less?"

These two sets of perspectives may become quite polarized. One women in her seventies commented that older women were usually married to husbands who did not approve of working wives! Statistics bear this out comment. According to the research of Reginald Bibby and others, Canadian women over seventy would have grown up and raised their children within a society where the vast majority of people did not think a woman should work outside the home if her husband was capable of supporting her (Bibby 1990, 57). By 1975, only a third of Canadians believed that. By 1995, fewer than 10 percent of Canadians held that view (and most who do are older Canadians [Bibby 1995, 95]). This simple question—should women work outside the home?—reveals vast differences in the experiences of women in our church. If one looks at the historical statistics, most older women would have stayed home and raised families. Today most women with children are working outside the home (Phillips and Phillips 1993, 33, 43).

For women raised in an era when women were not expected to work outside the home after marriage, the issue of whether women should or need to work may be viewed quite differently from those who grew up into a world where women were expected to do so. The claim that women need to work to support their families will also look different to women who reached adulthood in a time of scarcity compared to those who became adults in a world of many consumer goods. Some items not even available to older generations are now considered necessities. (Are these things really needed, some wonder, and do women really need to work so hard to get them.)

As one older woman pointed out, most of her adult daughters have "four or more jobs apiece and are constantly changing careers!" Sometimes younger women expressed frustration about the lack of understanding they sensed around this, and the feeling that demands were being put upon them. "I just don't have the available time," said one, "You like to bake. You know how to bake. You have time to bake. I have other things I *have* to do with my time!" These other time commitments often include family, work, and other volunteer commitments outside the church.

Older women responded immediately. They know, they said, that time is at a premium for younger women, especially those raising children. However they were quick to point out that this isn't the first generation of women to face pressures of time or to have too much to do. They too had led very busy lives, juggling families, housework, and some of them did work outside the home as well.

However, younger women often feel tugged between family demands and the church. When the church was the centre of community and family life, to be involved in church activities did not take one away from family, because most often the whole family was probably connected in some way. Now the church is only one social institution among many. And women, far more often than men, involve themselves and their children in congregational life without the involvement of their partners. But there are many other competing demands and interests. Women must choose among a variety of competing options, and often the choice is taken out of their hands by the choices of other family members. If the teens and children in their families feel like there's no place for them in the church, or if there are no functioning youth organizations, or if most of their peers are somewhere else, there is a strong pressure for the children to be elsewhere. Women end up as chauffeurs or are involved as volunteers for organizations other than the church.

In a more integrated society, a woman's volunteer involvement would have been visible to the whole community, and much of it would have revolved around the church. A young mother might have given leadership in a children's or youth program such as Explorers or CGIT, or helped out with vacation Bible school and summer camps. If she worked on any community charities, these too would have operated out of the church. Now, a woman might do the same kinds of things to support her community or the programs her children are involved in, but her work could be much more invisible to others within the church. All the older women know is that she's too busy to help with the tea. Younger women in turn say that the church makes too many demands, has unrealistic expectations, and has no idea what life is really like for women these days.

Divisive Issues

Differences between women run much deeper than issues of time and money. Generational differences have spawned a whole range of conflicts and disagreements, ranging from our opinions about sexuality to the changing role of women and men to the authority of scripture. While none of these issues is generational per se, there are definite generational trends. For example, the percentage of Canadians likely to approve of homosexual relationships varies greatly with age. According to a 1995 study, "18 to 34-year-olds held far more positive attitudes towards homosexuality than their parents or grandparents" (Bibby 1995, 72).

Our attitudes to family, sexuality, and the role of women and men in society, even our faith perspective, are all influenced by the experiences of our formative years so it is not surprising that we carry these differences with us; our values and attitudes may change over our lifetime, but those who study attitude change tell us that attitudes and values usually remain fairly constant. As a rule, we don't change very fast, or all that much. And so we carry these differences into all areas of church life. They affect our opinions about the language of worship, how we feel about the things the minister "does with her time," discussions about sexual orientation and ministry, or debates about the use of church space.

Different opinions and beliefs, if left to simmer for a while can easily lead to mistrust and suspicion, or what one woman in the workshops called "cross-generational spanking." That's when we start to verbally "beat others up for not behaving or believing the way we think 'they' should."

Such differences in perception sometimes cause tensions for women in the church. Sometimes it's more like a collision. Push a little deeper and some of the really tough issues start to emerge, issues much more difficult even than figuring out who is supposed to clean the kitchen. Issues of faith and theology, for example, seem to be a big points of contention. In the Naomi's Daughters workshops women identified things like how worship services are put together, how authoritatively they view the role of clergy or of scripture, or conflicting values about what is sacred.

Inclusive Language

As soon as one starts to talk about the sources of tension, inclusive language comes up. Whenever someone named it in a Naomi's Daughters workshop it was as though the group took a collective pause, a little gasp for breath. We all know that this is a big one! Worship, and especially the language of worship, has been a point of tension and division between women of different generations. Images that for some have become so liberating and empowering have, for others, been a source of pain and alienation. What for some women was like a window opening to the breath of the Spirit, felt to others as though something was being snatched away.

Throughout much of its history, Christianity has focused on images of God that are male (Father, Shepherd, Lord, King). The many feminine images of God that are in the Bible such as Mother, Spirit (which is always feminine in both Greek and Hebrew), or Wisdom (again always feminine in Hebrew) have not often been used. Even the more gender-neutral images and metaphors for God that are in our Greek and Hebrew Scriptures—rock, wind, fire, eagle, potter, gardener—have not held so central a place in the traditional language and worship of our church.

The issue of language became a sore point and a touchstone, and a place of deep division between women of the church. Women on both sides of the debate about inclusive language found themselves touched deeply. What has been named as a discussion about language is really about something far more fundamental. Inclusive language went hand-in-hand with naming the injustices in women's lives. The struggle for gender justice has had a long history. It began with the temperance movement—a struggle to protect women and their children from the poverty and violence, resulting from alcohol abuse, that were victimizing so many. It continued with the struggle to name women as "persons," the right to vote, and inheritance rights. But something reached a critical mass somewhere around the early to mid-1970s. For a whole generation, it no longer seemed right or reasonable that women should be excluded from professions such as medicine, engineering, law, or ordained ministry. It no longer seemed right or reasonable that women should be paid less than men or subjected to violence because of their gender. There had been women and men before who had held these views of course, but the balance shifted—these kinds opinions were no longer considered strange and marginal, or even aberrant.

The change of language that accompanied this change in consciousness was both symbolic and necessary. When I discovered that my male co-workers in the hospital food services department earned 20 cents more per hour for doing the identical work that I did, I knew that "men" did not include me. *Men* earned more money for doing the same work and therefore had to work fewer hours during the university term than I did to pay for books, fees, and living expenses. Thus the term "men" was no longer generic. It couldn't explain the sense of unfairness I felt at this imbalance. Language had to change in order to keep up with changes in perception. This was not just an intellectual or political decision. It occurred more at the gut level. The "old" language no longer worked—it no longer expressed what I wanted to say. I could not name myself as "man" or "brother" any more because I knew, in the blink of an eye it seemed, that I was not these things and never had been.

Marshall McLuhan knew already what many of us in the church had yet to discover. With every new technology comes the loss of an old technology. With change comes a loss. Of course "technology" in this sense doesn't mean just machines and technical innovations. It includes media and language. With every change, at all those levels, comes a loss of something else. There were, for certain generations, enormous losses associated with the move to more inclusive language for God and human beings. It wasn't just the loss of the familiar, I think, but a response to the much deeper changes in church and in society that inclusive language represented. I can see now that the loss was enormous, because I can see with what fierce determination so many in the church fought to hold on to what they believed was valuable and important.

To change language is to change to the core; it is to change the very essence of how reality is named. Change the name and you change the perception. Change the perception and you change the reality. When civil rights and anti-racism activists started rejecting the word "Negro" and embracing the word "Black" or, more recently," African-Canadian" they weren't merely changing the words. The word themselves represent a world view. Negro was the language of oppression, violence, discrimination, or self-hatred. Black and African are the language of pride, change, rights, justice, liberation, and heritage.

When women of a certain generation changed language in the church they were indeed shaking the foundations. Words can do that. No wonder those who loved the church, who had indeed worked a lifetime to sustain and nurture it, fought hard to hold onto the foundations. No wonder women looked at each other, as though across a chasm, not understanding what was going on.

Use of certain kinds of language in liturgy seems to trigger feelings of loss, resentment, and alienation. Exclusive use of the male pronoun for God or for human beings, for example, or prayers to Sophia or Holy Mother, seem to be red flags. Of course they all have strong biblical grounding and foundation in our religious tradition. Used in certain contexts, they seem fine. Used in other settings they seem somehow tainted by experiences of separateness and division. There is nothing "wrong" with them per se, and yet they seem to conjure up so much. "You just don't understand!" these words seem to declare to some. "You just don't value who I am and what I believe!" they shout back to others.

Inclusive language is just the tip of a very large iceberg. It has become almost a codeword—a short form way of talking about issues that have seemed at times almost too big to talk about. "Feminist thinking," one woman's way of describing this world of differences, has included changes in attitudes to work, sexuality, sexual orientation, power, authority—the changes are almost beyond comprehension. No wonder women in the church have difficulty understanding one another at times.

Does this spell doom and gloom for women in the church? Is the image of Naomi and Ruth—two generation of women supporting, loving, and accompanying one another into the future—simply a nice story from a bygone era? Certainly there are tensions, and without a doubt there are significant issues to address. And I think we will continue to need different groups to meet different needs and interests for women in the church. However, I don't think this needs to be divisive. I don't believe that we have to continue to live with the mistrust and misunderstanding, and even stronger—the conflict or sense of being let down or betrayed by one another. We need to work to rebuild trust and mutual respect. And we clearly have some work to do building bridges.

Peggy and Janet

Peggy Foster's moment of epiphany came in the supermarket, in the frozen food section of Zingers to be precise. She had been comparing prices on different brands of flour when it suddenly occurred to her to wonder how much frozen pies were. She looked in the freezer compartment. Peach pies, large ones, sold for $5.99. She almost fell over. They sold the pies at church, much smaller ones than this one, for $7.00. That meant that someone could walk into the Zingers any day they wanted and buy a homemade-style peach pie for $2.00 less, *and* get a bigger pie.

Peggy slipped a pie into her basket, looking over her shoulder to make sure no one from Martha's Circle was watching. At home, she baked it. Then she called Janet O'Neill. This would be the test. The phone rang three times before Janet picked it up.

"Hi?" There was a sound of the phone being dropped, followed by "Sorry. No, Meagan!"

"Sorry to disturb you," said Peggy. "I know you'll just be on your way out the door to get Blaise, but I wondered if you'd like to stop in on your way home. I have a peach pie just out of the oven, and I thought the kids might like to try a piece. You too, of course. I can't possibly eat a whole pie by myself," She realized Janet might think it rather odd of her to have baked it.

Janet hesitated.

"Of course, it will spoil the kids' appetites," Peggy Foster continued, "but there's lots of good vitamins in pie, in peach pie. And we'll have it with milk. We'll make it supper."

Janet laughed. "Sure, we'd love to," she said. "Oh, and thanks so much for the lily. I'm really sorry about the ones Meagan got to at church."

Peggy Foster remembered the lilies, but said it didn't matter. She had probably attacked a lily or two in her own day, she said cheerfully, wondering if this could be true.

Over pie and milk Peggy announced her decision. "I am giving up the pie bake next year."

"What?" Janet was truly astounded. "I thought you liked baking pies."

"No," said Peggy rather slowly, "I don't really. Fact is, I hate it."

"But the other ladies, the pies…?" Janet began. Guilt and fear edged into her voice. Was this a trap, to get her baking pies instead?

"If they enjoy it, fine, let them bake pies, said Peggy crisply, "and if they're having fun they won't miss me. But I've done the math. I figure if you take off the cost of ingredients we're making about $3.00 a pie. That works out to a rate of about 75 cents per person-hour, if you count all the cleanup and preparing the fruit, and the trip to buy peaches." She showed Janet her calculations. "It's not worth it. That's less than minimum wage."

"A lot less," Janet agreed.

"And, even if we didn't fill all the pie orders in a given year, people would still be able to get peach pies at Zingers. They're *almost* as good."

"I could tell the difference," said Janet generously.

"I couldn't," said Blaise, through a mouthful of pie.

"So, what I've decided to do," said Peggy, is what you offered to do when this whole thing first came up. I'm going to donate the cost of the ingredients, plus the 75 cents an hour, and I'm going to give up baking pies."

"What are you going to do instead?" Janet still couldn't quite believe her ears.

"Lots of things," announced Peggy. "I'm going to take more flowers to more people. Mrs. Cartmen, for instance. The only time I see her is at Easter. Why wait for Easter to deliver flowers? And, as for the peach pies, every so often I'm going to buy one, from Zingers, and invite you and the kids to have peach pie for supper."

"Yeah!" cheered Blaise.

"Yeah!" came a smaller echo from somewhere near the African violets.

Mrs. Newberry and Clare

When Clare got home there was a message from Jodi saying please call, I'm at my wit's end, and another from Mrs. Newberry asking could she please pick up the new curriculum package this week.

She called Jodi first. Another crisis with Rebekah, who had managed to get herself suspended for drinking during school lunch hour. There wasn't much Clare could say. She tried to reassure Jodi that she was doing all the right things, that Rebekah would come through it eventually. Then she called Mrs. Newberry.

"I would have left it at the office, but I figured it would be easier for you to get it from me in the evening," said Mrs. Newberry cheerfully. "And there are a couple of other things I'd like to talk about."

"It's a trap," thought Clare. "I go there. She tells me about the restructuring. I get roped into making the report to Council…" But she agreed to stop in and get the curriculum.

Mrs. Newberry, however, had other things on her mind, more important even than Sunday school restructuring. The list included ongoing concerns about the Lenten banner and, as usual, pies. "We just heard that Peggy Morrison is giving up pie baking next year," Mrs. Newberry began soberly. I know it doesn't mean much to you younger women but those pies raise over $3,000 a year and with the church deficit the way it is…"

Clare felt like screaming. Instead she slumped into a chair. "Mrs. Newberry," she said, "I don't know how to say this but I really, really, really don't know what to do about the pies. Anymore than I know what to do about the deficit or what to do when my best friend tells me her daughter just got suspended for drinking or any more than I know what to do with my own stupid, messed up, overworked life and I…" she paused and rummaged for a tissue in her pocket.

Mrs. Newberry looked mortified. "I'm so sorry. I had no idea. I'd never have mentioned the pies if I knew it would upset you so."

"It's not the pies," said Clare.

"No, I suppose it's not," said Mrs. Newberry thoughtfully. "I'd better put the kettle on."

Angie and Rebekah

Rebekah showed Angie how you could make a vortex in your coffee. "If you stir it hard before you add the cream it spins and spins and never mixes together," she said.

They were in the donut store near Rebekah's school. Angie had suggested getting together, after she heard about Rebekah's suspension.

Rebekah decided to get right to the point. "So, are you going to give me the church line about how unchristian I am, or the social-worker line about taking responsibility for my life, or the mum line about how could you do this to me?"

"None of the above," said Angie.

"So maybe it's the 'I'm very disappointed in you,' dad speech, or the older sister, 'how could you be such an idiot?' stuff."

"Nope."

There was a long silence.

"Mum is all set to cart me off to rehab," said Rebekah. "She's sure I'm a crack addict and an alcoholic. What she doesn't know is that everyone in my school drinks and this isn't such a big deal.

"Getting suspended, though, and lunchtime drinking?"

"It was only once, and she doesn't know the half of it really. Not drinking, because really, compared to a lot of people I don't drink that much, but the rest of my life I mean."

"Such as?"

"Such as, I hate my life!" Angie waited for Rebekah to continue. "I hate school. I hate how I look. I hate how if you go out with a guy he treats you like he owns you and can do whatever he likes with you."

"If we're talking violence, they can't you know…"

"Yeah, but they do."

9

Building Bridges

If the Naomi's Daughters workshops taught me anything it was that women in the United Church definitely want to build bridges across the generational divide. There is a genuine longing for connection. In places where there is conflict, there is also regret about the division and a desire for reconciliation. Women of the United Church are not, for the most part, willing to simply let this issue be. There is too much at stake.

At times, I sensed a frustration about where to begin. We want to "fix this" but we don't know where to start. The problems can seem too huge, and there may be many layers of accumulated misunderstanding. However, I think the workshops themselves provided a strong starting point, something that drew women closer together and increased mutual awareness. Women often said of the workshops, "we need more of this kind of thing," or "we need to do this again." Gathering to listen and hear one another's stories, experiences, and perspectives is a good place to begin.

Women in the workshops offered many other ideas about where to go from here. As I looked back over the pages and pages of notes and ideas, I became increasingly hopeful. It also became clear that in the task of building bridges there is we need to build a kind of "cross-cultural understanding." Women often used phrases like challenging the stereotypes, valuing diversity, becoming less judgmental, respect, learning about each other's differences, or dropping our prejudices. These expressions bear a striking resemblance to phrases used in the work to challenge ethnic, cultural, or racial stereotypes or prejudices. If we think of the generational differences as in many ways "cultural differences," perhaps some of the same strategies can apply.

Valuing Differences

The first step in bridge building, as with any bridging of cultures, is to ac-knowledge differences—differences in perception, differences in experience, and differences in values and beliefs. We have to *see* the differences in order to begin to view them as something positive. We don't always think alike or view the world in the same way. We don't have to be the same or do all the same things. Differences can be sources of conflict, but they don't have to be. Differences can also be gifts, gifts to use in our churches, gifts to celebrate. But first of all we have to be willing to acknowledge that differences exist. Often when confronted by differences there is a tendency for us to want to say "we're all really the same underneath." This can be a way of denying or covering up differences. It can devalue the gifts that we bring to our community precisely because we are different.

One of the mantras of anti-racism work is the phrase "different therefore equal." This phrase acknowledges differences as a reality but does not imply judgment—one better than another. Perhaps we have to learn to apply the same kind of standards when it comes to understanding one another as women, across the generations. We have to be able to say, "different therefore equal" in order to acknowledge that first of all, we *are* different and, second, this does not imply some preconceived notion of value or worth.

Facing up to our differences can also help relieve us of some of the fears we hold—fears of not being understood, of being "taken over" by another group, fears that this whole thing called church may fall apart, fears that we'll lose what we hold of such value in our churches or women's organizations.

Owning up to our differences can also free us up to the possibility that we don't all have all be in the same groups. It's okay for women to gather in separate groups to meet different needs. Separateness doesn't have to imply division or conflict. It can merely be a matter of choices and needs and interests. It may at times be necessary and even healthy, in order for a community to really honour the different needs, experiences, and gifts of its members.

In order to honour differences, we must be willing to let go of stereotypes and prejudices. As women in one of the workshops pointed out, "we must drop whatever stigma is attached to being 'too old and not able' or 'too young and not able.'" As women in the workshops said, "we must learn to respect each person's opinions and criticisms. We must stop belittling the younger women for offering new ideas and assuming that older people have no new ideas to offer. We must drop the stereotypes." There are differences but we still must avoid pigeonholing people by making assumptions that we already know everything there is to know about them because they are young, or old, or middle-aged. As long as we continue to think of differences between generations as acts of will, or defiance, we will continue to judge one another. You are not as I am, therefore you are not as you *should* be. Such attitudes will continue to create problems for us in the church.

Celebrating Commonalities

Once we have learned to acknowledge and value differences we can begin to identify those things that draw us together, our commonalities. Celebrating what we hold in common is not the same thing as saying we are all alike. Within a context that values our differences, it becomes possible to see and to value those things that draw us together.

Of course the most obvious commonalities is our commitment to our faith and to expressions of spirituality. It is easy for women to fall into name-calling and judgments about different expressions of spirituality—young women only want spiritual nurture and older women are so focused on the task they don't have any spirituality. This dynamic did come up a bit in the workshops. One woman called it the "Mary and Martha" syndrome. She was of course referring to Jesus' visit with his two friends. Mary is sitting with Jesus, talking about deep faith issues and Martha is stuck in the kitchen getting the meal ready, growing more and more resentful of her "lazy" sister.

To move beyond the "Mary and Martha" standoff, we must learn to honour different *expressions* of spirituality while identifying the underlying thread of commonality in our quest for spiritual nurture and spiritual expression. In the workshops, some older women talked about the deep spirituality they experienced "within the task." What looks like just "work" is much more—it is about community, about nurturing one another, and about faith. And often the spirituality that emerges in and through the tasks of baking, serving, or meeting is not compartmentalized. That is a gift. It is also a gift when women gather to reflect and nurture and deepen their sense of the sacred by stepping away from doing in order to be. They are, as Mary was, sitting in the presence of the sacred. Challenging the work ethic can call us back to what it really means to be the church. What sometimes gets judged as "avoiding work" can instil a deep commitment to supporting the institution that makes such spiritual nurture possible.

This leads to a second commonality—our commitment to the church. "We have a genuine concern for each other and for our church family," said women in one of the workshops. "We all have a commitment to the well-being of the whole community." Of course, there is a lot of misunderstanding, and even mistrust, about this. Part of it centres on the dynamic of seeing church as a given or something one should support or as an option and a choice on one's life. Again, misunderstanding can easily lead to negative judgments and perceptions of the other.

Women who view involvement in the church as a responsibility may view with suspicion those who view it as a choice. How deep is their commitment, really? If they chose this, they could just as easily un-choose it, and then where would we be? They may view this chosen commitment as only skin deep, as only self-serving. Seen from the perspective of those who have made a conscious choice to be involved with the church, things look very different. They may view with suspicion those who are "only here because they have to be." Are they really committed to being here out of a sense of joy and hope, or is this just a burden they have to bear? Are they just holding on to the way they think things are supposed to be, or are they really prepared to embrace the future?

These differences are also great blessings, however. Surely the gift of faithful and committed service, no matter what, is a gift worthy of high honour. Where would our churches be without those who hang in even when they are tired, even when they disagree with decisions the church makes, even when the church does not meet all of their needs? This is a gift of deep and committed love and service, which often has a quality of "till death do us part" about it.

And just as certainly, it is also a gift to the church that some have chosen it freely and without any sense of obligation because they believe church is relevant, important, and worth supporting within a culture that is saying precisely the opposite. What a gift that is to the church, to be chosen as a place where faith can be expressed, community can be built, and justice and compassion can be lived out. Woven together into the fabric of the whole, these different expressions of commitment to the church nurture the whole. One woman expressed it this way, "Young and old need to realize we are all working in the same family for the same God!"

Listening with Care

So, how can we move from places of fear and suspicion to places of understanding and appreciation that we are indeed working in the same family for the same God? "Listen to one another." That was how women in the Naomi's Daughters workshops summed it up. We have to get better at really listening to each other. Listening with integrity, really listening with openness to the other, means that we must learn how to suspend a tendency most of us have to judge what the other person says or insert our own experience too quickly.

To give a common example, a young woman talks to an older woman about how hard and stressful she is finding life at the moment, how much she feels the burden of having to juggle so many different things. Either aloud or silently, the older woman inserts her own judgment. "I worked harder than you did, life was stressful for me too, you have no idea how we struggled during the war…" Or, when the older woman shares her life experience, perhaps it is the younger woman who "interrupts" the communication with judgments. "You think you had it bad, but you have absolutely no idea what my life is really like, parenting today, working full-time, commuting, and I have to do it all on my own because my parents and grandparents are hundreds of miles away…"

We need to learn to listen with respect, without judging, moralizing, or giving advice. One woman in the workshop said what she wanted was a chance to share the wisdom of others without being told what to do, "knowing the boundaries of whose life is whose, and respecting one another's different choices."

We need to listen carefully and often, in order to develop a better appreciation for each other's different experiences. "We need to hear each other's stories," the women in workshops said again and again. What they meant, I think, was that we must give enough time and space and safety to one another to really hear the whole of who the other person is. We need to try to understand and remember the trials of each generation. "We don't necessarily 'all connect' through interests, life experiences, or schedules, but my hope is that we could still be present to one another," said one woman. Most of all, we need to have conversation across the generations, to hear one another's stories. We need to establish an empathy and interest in each other's lives, founded on respect and acceptance.

Telling Our Stories

The word storytelling itself helps to move us out of a judging frame of mind and into a listening one. After all, we are all storytellers in our daily lives as we relate and share anecdotes and experiences—the stories of our daily lives. And we can all appreciate the value of good stories. Our own faith heritage is also shared in the form of stories. Stories can build bridges in a way that explanations, arguments, and statements of belief simply can't. If I hear the story of a woman's life, as I did so often in the Naomi's Daughters workshops, I am invited into her reality. She tells me what happened to her, how she felt, and what she saw in the world around her. I can't tell her, you're wrong, you didn't *really* feel that way, because of course she did. Her story carries the truth of her life. It simply is. Storytelling moves us out of judging into a place of listening and, ultimately, of understanding.

The "safe space" we create to listen to one another is very important. Honesty is key, as is an atmosphere of safety and trust. All of us need to know they we aren't going to be judged or put down for what we say. Humour helps, partly because it takes the pressure off when things get tense or difficult, but also because humour itself is a way of forcing us out of the box. Humour has an element of surprise; often what makes us laugh is that the punch line is so different from what we expect.

The next task in the work of building bridges of understanding is perhaps the hardest one of all. You know that old trick of the nine dots. You draw nine dots, spaced equally apart in three neat rows, on a piece of paper. Then you ask someone to connect all nine dots with four straight lines, without taking her pencil off the paper. Is it possible? No, not unless you're willing to go outside the lines, to step outside the box. As long as we stay within the lines, limiting ourselves to what we perceive as the boundaries of the situation, we simply can't solve the problem. Often, it seems to me, we are so rigidly fixed in the rightness of our own way of seeing things that we cannot step outside the lines to see anything else. Our preconceptions—these are the limits, this is the way it must be—prevent us from seeing any other possibility.

The same thing applies to building bridges between generations. We can remain rooted in our own experience, refusing to step outside the box, or we can begin to view things from other points of view. We can begin to imagine how others might see things, even to start to see things from their perspective. As I watched women in the Naomi's Daughters workshops begin to appreciate and take on other points of view, I noted several stepping stones along the way. Listening carefully came first. Identifying and beginning to understand one's own perspective was a key factor: "I never knew I had that kind of attitude to

Start Here

change until now!" This paved the way to a realization that there are other different but equally valid points of view: "No wonder you would feel the way *you* do about change."

Using the Theory of Frameworks

The theory of generational differences can be an important tool for women in the church. I have come to believe that it can be very useful in helping us to understand and appreciate our generational differences. As with any tool of course, we have to be careful how we use it. We must be careful of overgeneralizations or stereotypes as we view the other. Stereotypes like "all Strivers resist change" or "all Challengers want change for the sake of change" can be most unhelpful. So can assumptions that because people are of a particular generation they will necessarily view the world through that framework.

At its best, the theory might help us understand one another and ourselves better. Asking ourselves questions like "what is my own basic attitude toward change?" or "I wonder what events in those key years of socialization shaped my generations assumptions about how the world is?" can help us identify our own framework filters a little more clearly. Knowing our own filters or frameworks leads to better understanding of other frameworks.

- How do I view change?
- How do I understand my role and responsibility to the church?
- How do I view authority?
- How do I understand my identity and role as a woman?
- Do I see moral values and beliefs as objective "facts" (this is true for all time) or do I look at them in relative terms (it's up to each person to figure out what he or she believes)?
- What my our basic attitude to money? To resources?
- How optimistic or not do I feel about the future, or about my role as an agent of change.

All of these questions, looked at from the perspective of frameworks of generations, can help us better understand ourselves and one another.

The more we understand about the differences in frameworks, the more tolerant we will become of the differences we encounter in everyday church life. One woman remembered an experience on a church financial committee of feeling as though the entire committee was saving up for some impending catastrophe. "Year after year they accumulated more reserves, which they never touched because 'you just never know what may happen.' I realize now that all the members of the committee except me were Strivers who had either survived the lean years of Depression and war, or were Calculators socialized in the years of recession and cutbacks. And there was I, stuck in the middle, wondering why we could never spend any of this money on mission or Sunday school furniture or anything!"

Respect for Different Viewpoints

Our understanding of different points of view may also make us more careful and respectful, as we work with others. I must remind myself that some of the people in a group I am meeting with are likely to see change as an unwelcome intrusion. I must be aware that I tend to view change as something positive, in which I expect to have a positive role. I must remember that some in the group may view change as inevitable but totally outside our control. Perhaps then I may be a little more careful about how and when I propose change. I may start to check or view more thoughtfully my own urge to initiate change at any opportunity. I may become more patient with those who oppose change. I may even begin to value and appreciate the role of those who work to conserve and hold on to what is of value in an ever-changing world.

We can bring a similar awareness of our attitudes towars our roles and responsibilities in the church. Many women of the Strivers generation see it as a duty and an obligation to support, work for, and participate in the church. They may be frustrated with others for not doing their share. Others resent the extra burdens. Understanding one another's frameworks might help us both to appreciate the loyalty, dedication, and labour generations of women have offered over many decades, and might help them to appreciate that church is something of such value to younger women that they have actually *chosen* it, not out of any sense of duty or obligation but out of a genuine valuing of what it is and what it represents.

Taking on the perspective of others, seeing the world from different points of view, also takes patience, and practice, and a kind of inner discipline to do the hard work of really valuing another person enough to step for a moment into her shoes and see the world as she sees it. Ultimately, also, I believe there is a spiritual dimension to this work. When we pray for another we cannot but take on the perspective of the other. We hold her in our hearts and, in so doing, we let her change us. When we let the Spirit infuse us as individuals and as communities, we are tuning in to the kind of Spirit-vision that will allow us to see others as God sees them and to see ourselves as God sees us.

Shared Action

And, finally, we need to act. We need to work together. Women in the workshops had all sorts of ideas about what this meant and how it might happen but they were very clear that sharing in a common task was vital to building bridges across the generations.

One place where women had already encountered strong points of mutual understanding and bridge-building was in pastoral care. They offered many examples of relationships of care for one another that had transcended age differences. Whether it was a group of older women helping a young woman who had recently given birth to triplets, visits to seniors or lonely shut-ins, or making casseroles for someone who was home sick or recently divorced, these experiences of care brought women in contact with one another. They came face to face with the reality of each other's lives, they developed trust in one another, and they came to love and appreciate one another.

Sometimes when women talked about shared work they did mention those big pie-baking extravaganzas or the like. These can indeed bring together women of all ages, and can be a lot of fun, but shared work didn't mean all the women had to get out there and work in the kitchen whether they liked it or not. It implied something much larger: a vision and commitment to something beyond ourselves. They mentioned outreach projects, social-justice work, concern about the environment, work with refugees, and involvement in the community. They talked about being the church in new and exciting ways and about living out the mission and ministry of the church. This wasn't just about work to support the institution through fundraising but the task of really being the church in the world.

This shared ministry isn't even really just women's work. Clearly it belongs to the whole community. But is an important forum within which women, and men, can build relationships of trust, understanding, and friendship. It doesn't mean everyone has to do the same thing, and do it all in the same way. It does, however, mean that we need a common sense of participating in the whole. As long as women see their individual contribution or work as compartmentalized, there will continue to be a sense of division. We must learn to see the individual pieces of work that we do fitting into the larger fabric of the church's ministry, as part of our shared work and shared commitment to the whole body.

Worshipping Together

The act of worshipping together is perhaps the biggest sign of our shared participation as one body in the church. It is also often the biggest test of our commitment to forging a commonality founded on respect for and valuing of our differences. Language—the language of worship and the theology underlying it—continues to push and challenge and test us.

What do we do as women in the church on either side of this great divide? We could continue to defend our right to use the language we prefer. We could argue and justify, from scripture, from tradition, from theology, and from our own experience. There is much in the Bible to support any number of different opinions about the "right" ways to speak to and about God. I suspect, in fact, that we will continue to have long and sometimes heart-wrenching conversations about these matters. There is nothing wrong with continuing to discuss and debate this. There's nothing wrong with good healthy argument, conflict even, as long as we are able to stay respectful and open to different points of view.

But what if we want to worship together across the divide? We could each insist on using our own "mother tongue," the language *we* prefer, knowing that we have not really succeeded in communicating. Like unilingual anglophones and francophones trying to converse, we could raise our voices louder and louder in the hopes that greater volume might increase the comprehension. Or, we can seek to find a common language.

I believe this common language does exist, and it exists in the realm of symbol, ritual, and story—the language of the heart, the language of the Spirit. It exists, this common tongue. We already use it; we need to use it more.

When we tell our own stories, speaking in the first person out of the experiences we ourselves have lived, we cannot help but speak in common tongue. When we open ourselves to the presence of the Spirit, we cannot do so divided. Someone places a bowl of flowers and a loaf of bread upon a table, while another lights a candle and invites the group to spend a few moments in silence. Or perhaps the group joins hands around a circle as they pray for God's Spirit to be with them in this gathering or in their going forth.

In these Spirit-filled moments, if we let ourselves simply draw breath and open ourselves to the presence of God's Spirit, I believe that God's Spirit will indeed be there. And, as in the infusion of the Spirit at Pentecost, there is a common tongue that transcends the language of division or the debates about the right language, the right ways to do things, or the right words to use. The Spirit can and does make of our separateness, one body. The Spirit speaks its own language. Often, it does not use words.

Moments of Grace

The event isn't exactly a fundraiser, and it certainly isn't a talent show in the traditional sense, but this annual mid-winter boost of ours brings together a vast range of ages and a remarkable combination of talent, humour, food, laughter, music, and the simple appreciation of being together in the same room. Older people tell stories or play for us; little ones join in animated group storytelling or share poems they have written. A Chinese member of the congregation, who very recently chose Christianity and this faith community, sings karaoke for us, in Chinese. The teens usually dance at these gatherings, in some creative form and to their music. This year they do an interpretive dance that begins with a teen party and moves to an appreciation of a spring sunrise. "There's more to life than this," they sing along with the refrain. The dance is both a critical examination of their own culture and a bridge from their generation to the rest of us. Any money we raise tonight will go towards a summer project of theirs—a two-week trip to help build a house for Habitat for Humanity. We close by standing in a circle, holding hands— babies and toddlers through to the eighty- and ninety-year-olds. We sing a blessing that is older than anyone in the room.

This story from my own congregation isn't about generations of women. It isn't a perfect solution to all the problems of the generations or the aging and attrition of the UCW. It is simply a reminder. Occasions like this help us to remember that much, probably most, of what we do in church is intergenerational. In our work, our worship, our celebrations, and most especially in our play, we continue to be remarkably adept at drawing together across a wide range of ages and life experiences. And most of the time it works surprisingly well.

The Church Tour

The church tour we did in the Naomi's Daughters workshop in Selkirk, Manitoba, stands out for me as one of those times when we really were able to celebrate what is working well, those moments of grace that have occurred in church parlours or around kitchen sinks. We walked through the church building, pausing at various rooms to recall what significant moments had occurred in that space—what work or recreation or ritual or community building had drawn women together across the ages. As we walked and talked, the stories simply poured out. In the kitchen, teens and seniors had made those fancy sandwiches together and countless groups of women, teens, and children (and not a few men) had rolled up their sleeves to wash the dishes. In the Sunday school rooms, teachers and teens and children had shared stories and sacred moments.

The upper hall recalled the wonderful community gatherings—funeral lunches, anniversary parties, teas, showers, send-offs, take-a-break morning programs for young mums. Then there was the pie room (where pies get cut in the annual bake off) which doubles as a meeting room for the Christian development committee (another intergenerational gathering of women). The sanctuary had the most intergenerational stories to tell, from Christmas pageants to music festivals, from communion to cleaning bees, but the lounge wasn't far behind. It housed the nursery—probably the most intergenerational gathering of all—as well as most of the church meetings, youth gatherings, Bible study groups, and volunteer groups. All of these gatherings were to some degree or another intergenerational, different ways of meeting the diverse needs of the community, and spanning the ages.

The church tour itself seemed to me to be a kind of celebration, a rejoicing in what we have been able to be and do as a multi-age community over the years. For all its difficulties, the church has continued to be one of the few places in our society where intergenerational contact still occurs. Of course there are conflicts and struggles, those things that draw us apart and cause us pain, but much of what we do meets the needs of many ages and stages. This isn't to say that we don't have room to grow, change, improve, and learn from our mistakes, but as a starting point for where we go from here it helps me to remember that we already are a cross-generational family. Like many families we have our moments, but we dearly love one another and we genuinely like to be together. Most congregations, I believe, have many very good examples of things that have worked well to bring women together across the ages.

The Church Tea

In the Naomi's Daughters workshops the church tea or equivalent was a source of criticism and concerns. However, in the very same churches where people complained, it was also a source of a great many wonderful examples of women of all ages working together on a common project and having a lot of fun in the process.

In one church, two very diverse groups of different ages collaborated on the tea. Each group met separately to do their own baking—the younger group found this to be a good stress-free time out and, because it was also a chance to be together and enjoy one another's company, it didn't feel like nearly as much work as having to do one more thing at home. Furthermore, the initative didn't come from the older group, which might have been perceived as yet another demand. The idea came from the younger women, who thought the older folk might need a helping hand. In another instance, a group of younger women created a slide show and sang songs of women's spirituality at a UCW tea. The slide show showed the faces of older women in the UCW, and as the pictures appeared on the screen the group sang "these are the women who throughout the ages…standing before us…" in wonderful tribute to this older generation. Again the initiative came as a creative idea, a way to honour and support and help, not as a demand or obligation.

Thinking back to what I discovered in the Naomi's Daughters workshops, there is an important insight here. Younger women are not motivated by a sense of duty or obligation. But given a clear need or an opportunity to show care and support or a chance to really make a difference in someone's life— these are things that will draw them out and draw generations together. And, as a side note to these examples, younger women also attended the teas in much higher numbers than usual because they knew their friends were going to be there. In many congregations the teas, pies, or community clean-up days or their equivalent, do seem to serve as a gathering point for all ages. And most women seemed to agree that one of the best ways to get to know another person is around a kitchen sink.

Mutual Care

The other big point of connection is found not in the women's groups or in the worship, but the care we offer one another. Most often this is informal and spontaneous. A young woman with triplets became the focus for an all-ages team in one congregation. Casseroles, phone calls, a kind word, an offer to baby-sit, or a note to say thanks—there are as many ways to offer care as there are United Church members. A great many of these contacts are cross-generational. What is even more noteworthy, a lot of these contacts begin as caregiving and evolve into ongoing friendships across the ages. Families adopt church "grandparents" or extra aunts. Isolated people find someone to talk to. Women with stressed-out lives find a bit of comfort and support. Again, these stories do not provide a solution to all the problems we face in our churches, but they can point us to some significant insights.

Not all cross-generational encounter is going to happen in formal meetings or groups. Most of it probably happens elsewhere, and very informally, across kitchen tables and outside on the church steps. If we try to measure our successes in terms of numbers of women in particular groups we are going to be sorely disappointed.

This leads to another important insight from the Naomi's Daughters workshops. Separate groups for different needs, interests, and yes, ages, is okay. In fact, it is probably necessary. It may even be one of our greatest success stories. Younger women may resist joining in the sense of taking out membership in a structured organization. They most certainly will resist a sense of having to be part of a women's group because it's their duty. But that doesn't mean they won't be part of an active and vibrant group, one that contributes in many different ways to the life of the congregation.

Of course, the UCW of former days also often had several different units operating in the same congregation. Many of these units were rooted in the two organizations that were merged by the United Church to form the UCW. Consequently the different units had different foci—some were more mission-oriented, some more study or prayer focused, others had more of a service-organization bent. And very often too, there were different units for different age groups. Perhaps because they were all UCW this didn't seem so contentious. Or perhaps it was a bit fractious at times and women just tend to forget those kinds of things. Whichever it may be, it's clear that different groups of women meeting in the same congregation is nothing very new.

Generations are different, and there are times when it is appropriate and important to gather separately. How that is viewed by the congregation and by the women themselves is an important factor in whether this can be a positive experience for all or a point of division and tension. If there is genuine respect for differences and a willingness to accept a diversity of groups and interests, groups often cohabit with great equanimity. What is more, they will often come together to collaborate around key events or shared interests. Where there is pressure or negativity: "You have to join our group and do things our way," tensions and fractures may emerge. The existence of separate groups is not, in and of itself, a sign of problems. Often it can be an indicator of a very healthy and alive congregation that has found creative ways to be a community that meets the diverse needs of its members.

Together across the Ages

Women also pointed outside their individual congregations to events that brought many women together across the ages. For twenty or more years, gatherings like the Banff Women's Conference and the Ontario Women's Conference have brought together women of many different ages and life experiences. Worship, music, workshops, mealtimes, and social activities clearly meet the needs of many different generations. The key ingredients at these events are spiritual nurture, community, challenging content, and time apart. Rarely do women go for an "intergenerational experience" per se, but they certainly encounter that in the process. In the Naomi's Daughters workshops, when I asked women what they most *enjoyed* doing with women of other ages, these events or ones like them were mentioned time and again. A retreat or conference format seems to be a good one for helping women step out of their separate age groups into a more common experience. Women attend in large numbers and they seem to have a good time.

Women in the Naomi's Daughters workshops had many new ideas—things they thought they'd like to try, ideas they thought others might find worth exploring. They talked of gathering to hear each other's stories, and taking more time just to listen to one another's different life experiences. It seemed in some ways as though the Naomi's Daughters workshops had struck a cord. They had heard stories from one another, and it had whetted their appetite for more. They had all sorts of suggestions for venue and lots of ideas, too for the kind of food they would serve! Food it seems, will always play a big part in gatherings of women. Many also talked of taking the storytelling out into the whole congregation—there are other bridges to build, they said, not just between us as women but as a whole community. Storytelling would be key.

And when they said storytelling, they didn't just mean sitting in a circle talking—they talked about photo projects, church history projects, story quilts, slide shows, dance parties, and costume events. One group suggested asking women to imagine their life experience as clothes strung out on clothesline. "Give them a large piece of paper and crayons and ask them to draw the key experiences of their life, and label those experiences." There was an almost endless list of creative possibilities for discovering more about who we are and what our lives have been like.

And women also suggested all sorts of other things they'd like to do together—mission and outreach projects, learning events on such topics as Earth Day, violence, awareness of issues in the lives of children, anti-poverty, and multiculturalism. The ideas ranged from the purely fun to much more serious and challenging topics. In these events too they wanted to share food and involve different ages and cultures and genders. They wanted children to be there. They wanted the whole community to come together. They wanted, they said, the whole diverse range of who we are as a church.

In all the brainstorming of new ideas, never once did the women mention creating a single ongoing women's group for all ages. In some instances they explicitly said this was not what they wanted. I think this is significant in several respects. It says to me that if this is the model or vision we have for the "future of women's work in the church" we are being far too limiting. There is great potential for women to relate, work, share, and celebrate across the ages but forcing this into a single box could well kill the creative spirit alive in our churches. We need to look to new ways of working, new visions and possibilities, rather than simply imagining that "women's work" will continue on as it always has. It is not likely that we will succeed; it is quite likely that most women don't even want this. And, in the words of the song the teens chose for their dance at my home congregation's community event, "there's more to life than this."

The Meeting

Lucy was the last person to arrive at the meeting. By the time she got there, the three groups had pretty much arranged themselves. Martha's Circle sat in an arc facing Spirit of Sophia. The youth group sat a little to the side, not quite in the circle. Clare Douglas and Mrs. Newberry had been appointed chairs for the meeting. They sat beside each other at the head of the circle, if circles can be said to have a head. Lucy slipped into an empty chair between Joanna and Mrs. Norris.

Each group had been asked to bring snack items to share. Lucy smiled inwardly as she looked at the laden coffee table. Each group's snack was as identifiable as if it had been labelled. Donut holes and cans of cola from the youth group, grapes and store-bought low fat carrot muffins from Spirit of Sophia, home-made banana bread and lemon squares from Martha's circle. The groups all had their distinctive dress codes too, she thought, from the vests and flared jeans of Angie, Sylvie, Michelle, and Rebekah (Lin had band that night) to the precise sweaters, jackets, and earrings of Martha's Circle.

Mrs. Newberry cleared her throat to begin. "Good evening ladies, she began. Clare Douglas and I have agreed to start this off," she said, glancing at a piece of notepaper. "These are the agenda items: the memorial flag, the annual pie bake, the kitchen cleaning, and use of the ladies' parlour by the girls in the youth group." She glanced at Clare for confirmation. "Well, the banner *and* the memorial flag," Clare corrected.

"Right," said Mrs. Newberry. "And before we begin, Clare has some general instructions for you."

Clare's general instructions consisted of a little pep talk on listening to one another and everyone trying to keep an open mind. Lucy promised herself she'd try, in spite of the fact that she, and probably most of the rest of the women in the room, wished she was anywhere else but here.

The use of the ladies' parlour was surprisingly easy, once the concerns about pop on the couches were allayed. The youth group gave small thumbs up signs to one another. The issue of the memorial flag versus the banner, however, proved more problematic. Anne tried to explain how the banner came out of an understanding of resurrection; the women dancing were rising up out of the ashes of violence and injustice in women's lives. Camille gave a small speech on how little younger generations understood about the sacrifices that men had made to save our freedom. But it was clear the debate was going nowhere fast.

"I lost my youngest brother in the war," said Thelma Norris tearfully.

"I lost my youngest sister to violence," said Joanna very softly.

There was a long silence. Finally, Rebekah Morrison put up her hand. Angie glanced over, wondering what she would say.

"I was thinking," said Rebekah, "that our church, well, probably there's room for two memorial flags isn't there. The banner and the flag, well, it's kind of like remembering two different things, two different kinds of violence I mean. I'd think we should vote for both of them."

After that the pies seemed, well, like a piece of cake. Martha's Circle explained that they were only able to make a hundred and fifty pies this year, and they didn't want to make anyone feel guilty but that was that. With Peggy not baking this year that was all they could manage. And Spirit of Sophia said fine then. And then Martha's circle wondered rather pointedly about the deficit and how the church would keep running.

Once again the youth group broke the impasse by suggesting raising the price of the pies to $10—like the oil producers and supply and demand—fewer pies, higher cost. Peggy did a quick calculation and said that even at $10 a pie they'd still be short. Camille had the idea of publishing the difference in the bulletin and asking the whole congregation to just put in a bit more offering the week the pies were sold to make up the difference.

And then, all that was left was the cleaning of the kitchen. Once again the youth group stepped in to solve the dilemma, when they volunteered to clean the kitchen once a month as a fundraiser. "We'll clean the kitchen. The church can pay us out of the maintenance budget. We'll use the money to help fund our Habitat for Humanity project this summer," they explained. Somehow this didn't seem to Clare all that different from simply paying Ed for a few more hours since the caretaking budget would still pay for cleaning the kitchen. Yet, as she thought about it, in a way it was different. Martha's circle might be hesitant to splurge on extra caretaking costs, but were quite happy to help out the youth group with their project. They all agreed to recommend to Council that the youth group clean the kitchen.

Then Clare gave a small word of thanks for coming and Mrs. Newberry said they would close by saying the Lord's Prayer, using whatever words they liked. This made the youth group giggle. Mrs. Norris wondered what words *they* were planning to use, and by the time they got through the prayer, everyone was giggling. "Probably all that pent-up tension," thought Clare.

"I just hope the Good Lord doesn't mind," said Mavis with a chuckle.

Clearing the Way

In order for there to be more "moments of grace" there are certain things that we must do as a church that go beyond simply building bridges of understanding. To truly connect and honour the diversity of all ages in the church, we also have to knock down some walls and remove some of the structural obstacles that serve to keep women separated and in conflict.

Lightening the Load

The church has, over the years, become heavily dependent upon the contribution women have made financially and in the care and maintenance functions of running a church. Everything from catering funeral lunches and special events to furnishing Sunday school rooms has often been left up to the women. The UCW has contributed an enormous amount of time and money to keep the church going and to fund its mission in the world. Smaller and smaller groups of increasingly older women are shouldering that burden. When Nellie McClung talked about the light work of lifting the mortgages being left up to the women, she was pointing satirically just how big a load it is that women have carried. Demanding or expecting that younger women will step in to fill the void will only increase a sense of alienation they may already feel. When women say they're doing all that they can, or more, we have to trust them. Letting women who have been carrying this load simply go on doing so until they drop with exhaustion will also only continue to fuel their sense of being overburdened, unsupported, and unappreciated. When women say they can't go on forever and need some help, we have to listen to them. Clearly, we have to lighten the load for all of us.

Removing the burden placed on existing UCW groups can take different forms in different contexts. Maybe a tea needs to become an event sponsored by the whole congregation or maybe it doesn't in fact have to happen. Being prepared to let go of some things could create an enormous sense of relief if the only reason something is being done is because people feel they should. Maybe we have to look at new and different ways of raising money.

Fundraising events don't in fact usually generate large amounts of money, particularly if one looks at the number of volunteer hours and donated goods involved. That doesn't mean they aren't important or that we shouldn't do them. But we need to ask some key questions about them. Is this rewarding? Do we really want to do this? Does it build community? Is it worth it to us to make this kind of time investment? We need to start to weigh the importance to the congregation of different kinds of events, and to consider whether there are other ways of meeting the community and social needs of the congregation and generating funds.

The whole congregation needs to take responsibility for its financial needs rather than becoming overly dependent on women's organizations to carry this. Perhaps some people really would prefer to donate money than bake a pie, but, if that's the case, it isn't only the women who should be asked to help out! Maybe some groups of women really do value the experience of baking all those pies, in which case the congregation should honour this important contribution. But that doesn't mean everyone has to bake, or even eat, those pies. We may have to look at other ways of raising funds, new ways to challenge and inspire people to help support the mission and ministry of our churches. I am not at all afraid for the future in this regard, having seen time and time again that, when people are excited about the creative ministry of the church in its own community and in the wider world, they come forward to support it.

Easing the burden on already overburdened women, and men, in our churches, may also mean we have to look at other things besides the women's groups. Churches can suck people dry. I hear many people complaining about the endless demands and requests that churches make upon them. We can accuse them of being lazy and make our demands more vigorously, or we can rethink what we are asking of them and why. Every time we hold a meeting or ask someone to do something, we need to ask ourselves questions about the use of that person's gifts. Are we asking for a gifted individual or will any warm body do? If the latter, we need to rethink the task. Will it really honour and use the gifts of the people involved, will it feed them spiritually, is this really needed, or is it just "because we always have this particular committee meeting" or this is what we have always done? We need to examine the things we do more critically. What need or ministry is being served by this task? How well does it use people's gifts? How important is it in God's service?

We need to rethink how much time we ask people to spend in meetings. Do they really want to be there or do we have to drag them kicking and screaming? Again, if the latter, is that a really good use of people's energy and resources? I know one congregation that simply cancelled half its meetings. Instead of meeting monthly, all committees met alternate months. The congregation found that since most committees were spending most of their time reporting on what had happened between meetings, the main outcome was simply a reduction in the amount of time people spent in meetings. The same amount of work still got done and people were more willing to serve on committees that only met four or five times a year.

Every time we hold a meeting, I think we need to ask ourselves if all the people present really need to be there, or if there are other ways to do what needs to be done—a letter to share information, for example, a quick check-in after church on one item, a two-person meeting. Every time someone suggests creating a new committee or task group, we need to ask if there's another way to do the work. Sometimes we think a committee needs twelve people because that is what the number has always had. Lightening the load may mean getting it done with five or three. Lightening the load for women means lightening the load for all of us in our overburdened churches. Lightening the load may free us up from the resentment of being asked too often for too much or from doing more than we really can or want to because of duty, and allow us to do more creative things with the spiritual gifts God has given our communities. Lightening or sharing the load may give us more energy for what really matters. It can be a way of creating space in our collective life, spirit-space where God's Spirit has room to breath and move.

It seems to me that we are very busy, sometimes too busy, as a church. Our strong work ethic makes it hard for us to let go of the things we have always done and the ways we have always done them. It can make it hard for us to take time apart for spiritual nurture, for prayer, for letting go, for letting God's Spirit move in and among us.

Jesus modelled a path of taking time out for prayer, for time with God, for desert or Sabbath time. In the conflict between Mary and Martha, Jesus spoke of the "better part" that Mary had chosen (Lk. 10:42). I think he did so not to belittle Mary, not to denigrate the contribution women make through hard work, but to hold up for us as women, and for us as a church, another possibility. We don't always have to be busy. We should not always be working. Sometimes our work in itself can block the deeper work of God's Spirit, can disempower us, can wear us down, can lead to petty conflict, and can stifle vision and creativity.

We need Sabbath time to restore our souls, to rekindle our awareness of God's presence in us and in one another. We need an ethic based not so much on hard work as on Spirit-filled daily living. We need to rest, to breath, to wander into the desert alone or with other pilgrims. We need to let the Spirit lead us into new paths.

Once we've done that, it will be easy for groups of women (and men and teens) to meet "just" for spirituality or nurture and for other groups to bake pies or hold teas or host banquets simply for the delight and pleasure it gives them and others. We won't have to get into the same kinds of arguments about which are more important. We will discover that all kinds of gifts and faith responses are an important part of who we are. We'll uncover a whole lot of other gifts that we never knew were there.

Once we have eased the burden, we will have freed up space to really connect. We will be able to celebrate being with one another. It will be easier to take time to tell stories or share perspectives. We'll have time to really talk with one another about those hard and conflict-ridden topics. And we'll have energy leftover to laugh and just to be together.

The Bus

Jodi and Peggy loaded the boxes of groceries into the back of the bus, arranging people's bags around them.

"Do you think we have enough food?" asked Peggy.

"I think we've got enough food for an extended hurricane," said Jodi. "I just hope we haven't forgotten anything major."

"Yeah, like the pizza!" said Lin voicing the youth group's concern.

The three women's groups, Spirit of Sophia, Martha's Circle, and the youth group, were taking a weekend jaunt to Camp Obilong. It would be too cool for swimming, but they figured between games (which the youth were organizing), walks in the woods, cooking meals, and just chatting by the fire, there would be plenty to do.

"Whose wild and crazy idea was this anyway?" asked Mavis cheerfully, as the bus pulled onto the main highway. "Peggy's I think," said Lucy looking around the bus.

Peggy was crammed in a seat with Blaise and Meagan O'Neill. Both children were vying furiously for her attention. She didn't seem to mind, in fact, it looked as if she was quite enjoying herself.

Jodi and Thelma were deep in conversation, as were Angie and Rebekah. A couple of the other women were settling in for a short nap. Some were just enjoying the view.

Most of the youth group and the rest of the kids were at the back of the bus eating chips and singing "Little Rabbit Foo Foo" at the top of their lungs.

"It's going to be an interesting weekend," said Lucy.

Mavis nodded. "I just hope the camp is big enough for the pack of us."

"We'll give the youth their own cabin deep in the woods," said Lucy.

"I think we should give Mrs. Newberry and Clare a separate cabin too," said Mavis, especially if they're going to keep that up all weekend. Lucy glanced over. Mrs. Newberry and Clare were having an intense debate about the feminine side of God. It was a conversation they had started some weeks ago. It didn't look as though they'd be finished anytime soon.

Memories and Hopes

Each spring the UCW of First United Church hosted a very elegant spring tea.

We had tickets made up, and would invite special people to open our tea. It was a very busy time with so much preparation. Ruth Chaffey was known for her crafted table centrepieces that were for sale. Other ladies would decorate the hall beautifully.

The silver tea services were polished up the night before, and silver sugar and creamers were brought in for each table. We even had white paper doilies on the cake plates and under the best china cups. I especially remember one lady bringing in her iron and board just to remove the folds from the laundered tablecloths. We were very particular!

Then we produced mountains of sandwiches and cakes. Do you remember Mabel Stewart would bring those pinwheel sandwiches of cream cheese with cherries in the centre? There would be egg, ham, and salmon sandwiches. Buttered raisin bread, squares, and butter tarts. Sometimes we served Jell-O squares with fruit.

There were greeters at the door and honoured guests took turns to pour at the centre table. Of course, we wore our Sunday best, which included hats and gloves.

Friends were invited—often from other churches—and it's a well-known fact that the teas would be compared and judged!

What bustle and what hard work! But what enjoyment and satisfaction, with some wonderful memories!

—Ila Turner, First United Church, Ottawa, 1998

Do you remember? If you are old enough, I'm sure you do. Not just the mountains of sandwiches at the spring teas, but also the mountains of used clothes to help someone in need somewhere in the world, the mountains of documents studied and books read, the mountains of mashed potatoes served and coins collected. In local congregations women worked and ministered with resourcefulness, commitment, and creativity—doing everything from washing the curtains and scrubbing the floors to visiting the sick and feeding the hungry. An ancient piece of Chinese wisdom says that "women hold up half the sky." It would be safe to say that women in the United Church have held up at least half the church! In 1962 women's organizations in the United Church were funding half of the overseas mission of the church and about a third of the home mission work. When the UCW was formed in 1963 and the Woman's Missionary Society disbanded, the WMS transferred 1.6 million dollars to the general funds of the United Church.

In an era when women were not permitted onto the Session or Stewards, or into the larger arenas of church life, and had no part in the church's decision-making, women contributed hour upon hour of volunteer labour to build churches and fund mission and ministry in the world. The church was also one of the few places where "women's work"—baking, making and serving meals, sewing for the bazaar, etc.—was rewarded with money. Not that the women kept it for themselves, but they did get "paid" for their work.

But this rich legacy has not all been about work. It has provided rich bonds of community, care, and friendship that continue to this day. The careful study, spiritual reflection, learning, and prayer have provided rich nourishment and challenge not just for women but for the whole church. The treasured traditions, from silver tea pots to the loving creations of warm, comfortable spaces in our churches continue to transform our church buildings from empty shells into places of overflowing with the warmth of community. Most of our buildings have some sort of gathering spot that was, or still is, "the ladies' parlour," and it's usually the most comfortable spot in the church.

The statistics and demographics of our churches, and of the traditional women's organizations, suggest that all this is changing. Some even predict the end of the UCW, as more and more local units disband. Changing roles for women in society have meant that women are no longer barred from church decision-making bodies. In fact, in many churches they are in the majority on boards and committees. Changing times mean that many women no longer have the time or inclination to contribute endless hours to hosting church suppers. And rapid social change has created generational gaps in understanding, attitudes, values, and world view between women of different ages. Have changing times really spelled the end of this rich heritage of women gathering to work and worship, laugh, pray, wonder, eat, share…?

As I think back to the laughter and vitality of the Naomi's Daughters workshops, I am anything but pessimistic. The energy, the storytelling, the sheer delight in coming together attest to a strong and dynamic future for women coming together in our churches. The future will be different from the past, I believe, but many of the same elements will be present.

Women will continue to contribute to the support and ministry of the church. Women will continue to act as leaders and decision-makers. They will continue to challenge the church as well as to support it. In the past, women carried out much of their ministry and made their contribution to the life of the church from within the traditional women's organizations. Now, as women are increasingly integrated into the larger structures of the church, they will share their unique gifts, talents, and insights within the larger body of the church.

Churches, in turn, will pick up an increasingly larger share of the financial and support functions that were formerly carried out by the women's organizations. They will have to, or the work won't get done. Since I firmly believe our churches do have a rich and dynamic future, I believe the whole church will find ways to do what has been traditionally left to the women. They might not do it in quite the same way, but the work will get done.

Women will continue to meet and work together, but much more of this encounter will take place in mixed groups—on church committees, at community events, at worship, on mission and outreach projects, and in pastoral care.

However, I think women will also continue to gather together as women. We will do so less and less as ongoing groups or fixed organizations with a complex ongoing structure. We will meet more often for short-term events—a study group, a retreat, a women's conference, a shared worship experience, or an outreach project. Our structures will be lighter and less labour intensive, with less need for formal leadership roles of secretary or president.

There will be more variety in our gatherings and more choices offered. Sometimes we will meet in mixed age events; sometimes we will meet in separate age groups. The essential elements, though, will all be there—friendship, vision, commitment, care, laughter, and, as always when women gather together, good food! The Spirit will be with us. As diverse in expression and movement as we women are, the Spirit will be there, creating something new, moving us along, and shaping us, in all of our diversity, into God's holy people.

Part II
Naomi's Daughters Workshops

Introduction to the Workshops

The workshop tools were developed to help women of different ages in the church come together to build a common understanding, to develop deeper respect and trust, and to discover new ways that they can work, worship, and be together as women in the church. The aim of the workshops was to build bridges of understanding that would help women in the church of different age groups understand one another and work, worship, learn, and "be the church" in new ways.

The workshops, and particularly the timeline and storytelling activities, were tested with groups of women in many different settings—rural, urban, small-town and suburban—and in different parts of Canada. Group sizes varied, as did the culture and ethnic background, life-experience, and context of the women. Out of these "testing ground" experiences, the workshop elements were refined and combined into the workshop outlines that follow.

In the process of developing the workshops, no two events were exactly the same, and even though the plans below might look somewhat "fixed" you will probably find that no workshop you do is exactly the same as any of these outlines. Stories and conversations will be different, the agenda will bend and flow to meet the needs of your particular group, and the learning and action that comes forth also will be unique to your group and setting. As you plan your event, be sure to adapt these tools to suit the needs and interests of your group.

Purpose

The workshops were developed with a common purpose: to build bridges of understanding, respect, and action between women of different age groups in the church. There are different reasons women might choose to participate in a workshop on this topic:

- they might want to learn more of one another's stories
- there may be separate groups of women within the same pastoral charge looking for an opportunity to have a common experience learning and sharing with one another
- they might be women within an existing group who are looking for a new program idea
- there may have been a sense of distancing or tension between age groups within a congregation, and women may be looking for ways to build greater mutual understanding

- there may be no active women's groups, and this might be an opportunity for women to gather together for a one-time event or to begin to build a group.

Whatever the reason, the workshop offers an opportunity to:

- share stories of women's lives and experiences
- learn more about the perspective and experiences of different generations of women
- build deeper mutual understanding
- explore differences and commonalities between women of different age-groups
- identify blocks and obstacles to common understanding or shared work
- build bridges of action and shared work
- celebrate strengths, things that are working well, and the work that women have done together
- create new resources or liturgy or new program plans
- plan next steps or other action together
- worship and pray and experience the presence of God's Spirit

The Group

As I tested workshops in different contexts, I found that the ideal group size for this learning experience is sixteen to twenty-four women. Much larger, and the storytelling or sharing of experiences becomes too long and drawn out. Much smaller, and there is not enough diversity of age and experience to really gain a deep appreciation for different ages and perspectives.

If a large number of women are interested, consider holding two different events. If the group is too small, deliberately seek out and invite others, or ask those who are interested to invite other women they know. Or, consider holding the event at a later time when more women may be able to participate.

In my experience developing these workshops, I found that the wider the age-range the more positive the outcome for the women who participated. It was particularly important, and particularly difficult, to include younger women in the events. There are a several reasons for this. Younger women do tend to have busier lives with more pressures and less time flexibility; often they are juggling multiple responsibilities—jobs, children, partners, or care of older relatives. Some of the younger women who did participate in the workshops to develop this book did so initially with a sense that they didn't really have time for this, although afterwards they felt very grateful for and energized by the experience. The very youngest women in the church also have many other competing activities and interests—for them, church is but one choice among many other options. And it is a choice most of their peers are *not* making. For youngest women, time at such an event is largely time away from their peers and friends, a choice that some were reluctant to make.

Things that may make it possible for more women, of a variety of ages, to participate:

- providing on-site child care for women with young children
- providing a simple meal as part of the event, but something that does not cost a lot for the women either in terms of time preparing food or financially
- carefully consulting with women about time of day and location—evenings are often hard for older women; weekdays may be impossible for women who are employed outside the home
- making special invitations to women, especially younger women—invite existing groups or friendship circles, invite mothers and daughters, grandmothers and granddaughters, aunts and nieces, leaders and teenagers; make sure that younger women know that others their age will be participating
- offering transportation for women who need it
- ensuring that the meeting space is fully accessible to all women
- inviting women to help share leadership

Leadership and Planning

Planning Team
A planning team of three to five women would be ideal. You might divide leadership and preparation responsibilities among the team, or some team members may prefer a "behind the scenes" while others take up-front leadership. It would be helpful if all members of the team have a chance to read the workshop outline and chapters 1, 5, and 6 before you begin planning.

Read the outline

Materials and preparation needed are indicated in the workshop outline, in italics, before each session activity. Make careful note of the supplies and preparation needed. For all workshop sessions you will need material for writing notes—whiteboard or flip chart, and paper and pens for participants. You will also need to create a worship centre: a small table with candles, cloth and other objects you choose can create a visual focus for worship. For longer workshop outlines you will also need to consider the need for food and beverages.

You will need

Photocopying
Workshop handouts and resources for worship and ritual can be photocopied for use in the workshop. Please do respect copyright—photocopy only those materials that indicate that permission to photocopy has been granted. If you wish to have participants read the book, as in the six-session study option, arrange to purchase copies in advance. Please inquire through your Book Room for large quantity discounts.

Permission to photocopy

Timing

Times for the workshop outlines are approximate. If you have a small group, things may move more quickly. Larger groups tend to take longer for conversation. As you plan for the event, consider what you might do if things move quickly and you have extra time. Which activities will you drop if you need to, for reasons of time? Be sure to save time at the end of the event for evaluation and closing, even if you do not do every activity you planned.

The times indicated in each of the four workshop outlines can be varied—add or move breaks to fit your group needs. You may want to add or delete certain activities. The workshop outlines are a guide to aid your planning and I encourage you to adapt the plan to fit your group.

Five Workshop Options

Five workshop formats are presented, along with sample session outlines.

Option 1

A Half-Day Event
such as a Saturday afternoon (3 to 4 hours)

5–10 min.	**Welcome and Gathering** Use the Introduction A to gather the group, welcome everyone, and explain the purpose of the gathering.	**Component 1** *Introduction A* page 140
10 min.	**Opening Worship** Use one of the shorter worship openings, such as "God of All the Ages," "Look into My Eyes," or the "Invocation of the Spirit."	*Resources for Worship and Ritual* pages 170–171
30–40 min.	**Bible Study:** **Reflecting on the Story of Ruth and Naomi** Use the shorter option in each step of the Bible study. Use steps f and g if you have time.	**Component 2** *Bible Study* pages 142–144
75–80 min.	**Storytelling with Timeline** Use the outline provided for steps a, b, and c. You will need to keep close track of time, and carefully time the sharing of each age group so that there is enough time for all groups to share. If you have five groups you can allow about 8 minutes per group, or up to 10 minutes if you have four groups.	**Component 3** *Storytelling with Timeline* pages 145–148
15–20 min.	**Break** Consider offering beverages and a simple snack such as fruit to boost energy. You may wish to have a break somewhere in the timeline process, rather than waiting until all groups have shared. Time the break carefully; in larger groups it can take 3 or 4 minutes to reconvene and get started.	

30 min.	**Storytelling with Timeline (step d)** Use the reflection questions provided in the workshop outline, step d. You will probably not have time for the longer options.	page 148
30 min.	**Generations of Women in the Church** Use the Group Discussion B provided in the workshop outline. You will not have time for the fishbowl activity (Option A).	**Component 4** *Generations of Women in the Church, Group Discussion* page 150
15–20 min.	**Moving On** Invite women to talk for a few minutes about what they have discovered in this time together. Brainstorm some possible next steps and record ideas on newsprint. Suggest that the workshop planning group and any others who may be interested might meet to discuss them. Appoint someone to convene this meeting. Use the Evaluation in the workshop outline, Option C.	**Component 8** *Evaluation* pages 157, 168
5–10 min.	**Closing Worship** Use a closing prayer or blessing from the options provided, such as "Ritual of Thanks," "Commissioning of the Spirit," "Shower of Blessings," or "Closing Prayer."	*Resources for Worship and Ritual* pages 175–176

Option 2

A Full-Day Event
such as a Saturday from 9:30–4:30 or a Sunday
afternoon and evening

15 min.	**Welcome and Gathering** Use the Introduction A to gather the group, welcome everyone, and explain the purpose of the gathering. Use Option B, Introducing Ourselves, from the workshop outline.	**Component 1** *Welcome and Gathering* page 140
15 min.	**Opening Worship** Use "Look into My Eyes" followed by the prayer "God of all the Ages" or the "Ritual of Lines into Circles."	*Resources for Worship* *and Ritual* pages 170–171
60 min.	**Bible Study:** **Reflecting on the Story of Ruth and Naomi** Use the outline provided. Use the longer options. Omit step g if you run short of time.	**Component 2** *Bible Study* pages 142–144
15–20 min.	**Break** This may be a good point for a break, or you may want to have a break during the timeline activity below. Consider offering beverages and a simple snack such as fruit or muffins to boost energy.	
60–80 min.	**Storytelling with Timeline:** **Generation-Shaping Experiences** **(steps a to c)** Use the outline provided. You will need to keep close track of time, and carefully time the sharing of each age group so that there is enough time for all groups to share. If you have five groups you can allow about 10 minutes per group, or up to 15 minutes if you have four groups. You may need to continue the sharing after lunch, depending on when you choose to eat.	**Component 3** *Storytelling with* *Timeline* pages 145–148

| 45–60 min. | **Lunch** | |
| | Keep lunch simple, with items that can be prepared well in advance with minimal cleanup, or have lunch catered. Some groups prefer a shorter lunch break so that the day ends earlier. | |

50 min.

**Storytelling with Timeline
(end of step c and step d)**

Finish the sharing from each group if you did not complete it before lunch. Use the reflection questions provided in step d. You will not have time for the longer option, step e.

page 148

15 min.

Generations of Women in the Church

Use the discussion process provided in the workshop outline, Option B. You will probably not have time for the Fishbowl activity (Option A).

Component 4
Generations of Women in the Church
page 150

Break

20 min.

Break when the group needs to do so, with beverages, fruit, etc.

50–60 min.

Visions and Hopes for Women in the Church

Use Options A and B in the workshop outline. Keep careful track of time (10 minutes to prepare skits, 5 minutes per group to present). Warn groups they will have to work quickly to put their skits together. It will in fact boost the energy of small groups to have a bit of time pressure, so don't worry about pushing them a little.

Component 5
Visions and Hopes for Women in the Church
page 151

20–30 min.

Celebrating Our Common Work

Use Option C: Thinking about Our Sucesses. Probably you will not have time for the church tour (Option A or B) but if you do, it's easy to build it in. You will need to leave the last 45 minutes for the last part of the workshop.

Component 6
Celebrating Our Common Work
pages 153–154

20–30 min.

Moving On: Next Steps, Evaluation, and Closing

Do Option B of the outline provided. You will not have time to do Option A, Planning for the Future. Instead, you might brainstorm some possible next

Component 8
Moving On
page 157

steps and record ideas on newsprint. Suggest that the workshop planning group and any others who may be interested might meet to discuss possible next steps. Appoint someone to convene this meeting.

 Handout copies of the evaluation form. Use the evaluation process described in the workshop outline, Option C.

Handout 5
page 168

15 min.

Closing Worship
Use a closing prayer or blessing from the options provided such as "Ritual of Thanks," "Commissioning of the Spirit," "Shower of Blessings," or "Closing Prayer."

Resources for Worship and Ritual
pages 175–176

Option 3

A Weekend Retreat
(Friday evening to Sunday noon)

Friday Evening (2.5 hours)

15 min.	**Getting Started** Gather with music or a time of silence. You will probably want to use music and singing throughout the workshop, as part of worship, as a way to boost energy, or to gather back after breaks.	
10–15 min.	**Opening Worship** Use "Ritual of Lines into Circles" or "God of All the Ages."	*Resources for Worship and Ritual* page 170
	Welcome and Gathering Use the Introduction A in the workshop outline to gather the group, welcome everyone, and explain the purpose of the gathering.	**Component 1** *Welcome and Gathering* page 140
15 min.	(Optional) Use Option B: Introducing Ourselves, from the workshop outline.	page 140
25–30 min	From the workshop outline, use Option C: Hat Creations or Option D: Making Names for Ourselves, to help group members build community together.	**Component 1** *Community Building* page 141
15 min.	**Break** This may be a good point for a break, or you may want to have a break during the Bible study below. Consider offering beverages and a simple snack such as fruit or muffins to boost energy.	
60–70 min.	**Bible Study:** **Reflecting on the Story of Ruth and Naomi** Biblical reflection on Ruth and Naomi; use the outline provided. Probably you will have time for the longer options.	**Component 2** *Bible Study* pages 142–143

15 min.	**Closing Worship** Use "Closing Ritual with Ribbons."	*Resources for Worship and Ritual* page 175
	Saturday Morning (3 hours)	
15 min.	**Opening Worship** Use the "Ritual of Lines into Circles" or "Litany of Women's Lives through the Ages."	pages 170, 173–174
80–100 min.	**Storytelling with Timeline: Generation-Shaping Experiences (steps a to c)** Use the outline provided. You will need to keep track of time, so that there is enough time for all groups to share. If you have five groups you can allow about 15 minutes per group.	**Component 3** *Storytelling with Timeline* pages 146–148
15–20 min.	**Break** Take a break when the group needs one during or after the timeline activity.	
45 min.	**Storytelling with Timeline: Generation-Shaping Experiences (steps d and e)** Use the reflection questions provided the workshop outline.	Page 148
1 hour or more	**Lunch**	
	Saturday Afternoon (3 hours)	
45 min.	**Generations of Women in the Church** Use the Fishbowl activity, Option A. If you are running short of time, use Option B, Group Discussion.	**Component 4** *Generations of Women in the Church* pages 149–150
60–80 min.	**Visions and Hopes for Women in the Church** Use the activities described in the workshop outline Options A and C. Keep careful track of time (12 minutes to prepare skits, 7 to 8 min. per group to present). Warn groups they will have to work quickly to put their skits together. It will in fact boost the energy of small groups to have a bit of time pressure.	**Component 5** *Visions and Hopes for Women in the Church* pages 151–152
15–20 min.	**Break** Take a break, when the group needs one, during or after the visioning activity.	

| 60 min. | **Celebrating Our Common Work: Church Tour**
Take an actual or a virtual church tour using Option A or B described in the workshop outline. | **Component 6**
Celebrating Our Common Work
pages 153–154 |
| 30 min. | **Celebrating Our Common Work:**
Thinking About Our Successes
Use the discussion activity, Option C, to reflect on what you have discovered and learned so far. | page 154 |

Saturday Evening (2 hours)

| 60–80 min. | **New Creations**
This evening is a time of creativity. Explain the options available, divide into groups, and encourage the participants to have fun creating. Follow the activity outline. Explain that tomorrow morning will be a time for groups to and share what they have created. | **Component 7**
New Creations
pages 155–156 |
| 15 min. | **Closing Worship**
Use "Receiving the Blessings of Generations of Women" or "Litany for Naomi's Daughters" or a worship ritual created by the group. Close with singing or a time of silence with candles. | *Resources for Worship and Ritual*
pages 172–173 |

Sunday Morning (up to 3 hours)

15–30 min.	**Opening Worship** Use "Psalm of Thanksgiving" or a worship ritual created by the group yesterday evening. Have a time of singing, or silence with candles.	page 173
20–30 min.	Give groups a time to share with one another what they created yesterday evening.	
105 min.	**Moving On: Next Steps, Evaluation and Closing** Use the process described in the workshop outline, Planning for the Future, Naming Learning, and Evaluation.	**Component 8** *Moving On* page 157
20–30 min.	**Closing Worship** Use a "Litany of Women's Lives through the Ages" or a worship ritual created by the group last night. Close with singing.	*Resources for Worship and Ritual* pages 173–174

Option 4

A Six-Part Series
(six 2-hour sessions)

Breaks are not marked. You may wish to gather for coffee and muffins early in the session or end with a refreshment break or your group may wish to insert a break in the middle of your session.

Participants may wish to read the book as an accompaniment to this study series. They should read certain chapters before each session. The appropriate chapters are indicated in brackets at the beginning of each session outline.

Session 1
(Reading before the session: Introduction and Chapters 1 and 2)   pages 3–20

5 min.	**Opening Worship** Use "God of All the Ages."	*Resources for Worship and Ritual* page 170
10–20 min.	**Welcome and Gathering** Use the Introduction A in the workshop outline to gather the group, welcome everyone, and explain the purpose of the gathering. You may wish to use Option B "Introducing Ourselves" if people do not know one another well.	**Component 1** *Welcome and Gathering* page 140
70–80 min.	**Bible Study:** **Reflecting on the Story of Ruth and Naomi** Biblical reflection on Ruth and Naomi; use the outline provided. Probably you will have time for all of the steps.	**Component 2** *Bible Study* pages 142–144
15 min.	**Closing Worship** Use "Closing Ritual with Ribbons."	*Resources for Worship and Ritual* page 175

Session 2
(Reading before the session: Chapters 3, Stories II, Chapters 4 and 5)   pages 21–47

10 min.	**Opening Worship** Use the "Invocation of the Spirit."	*Resources for Worship* page 171
105 min.	**Storytelling with Timeline:** **Generation-Shaping Experiences** Use the outline provided. You will need to keep track of time, so that there is enough time for all groups to share. If you have five groups you can allow about 10 minutes per group.	**Component 3** *Storytelling with* *Timeline* pages 146–148
5 min.	**Closing Prayer** Use "Closing Prayer."	*Resources for Worship* page 175
	Session 3 (Reading before the session: Chapter 6, Stories II, Chapters 7 and 8)	pages 49–89
10 min.	**Opening Worship** Use the "Ritual of Lines into Circles."	*Resources for Worship* page 170
105 min.	**Generations of Women in the Church** Use the Fishbowl activity, A. If you are short of time, use the discussion questions from Option B instead.	**Component 4** *Generations of Women* *in the Church* pages 149–150
5 min.	**Closing Worship** Use "Ritual of Thanks."	*Resources for Worship* page 175
	Session 4 (Reading before the session: Stories III and Chapters 9 and 10)	pages 93–102
10 min.	**Opening Worship** Use "Psalm of Thanksgiving."	*Resources for Worship* page 173
105 min.	**Visions and Hopes for Women in the Church** Use the activities described in the workshop outline Options A and C. Keep careful track of time. Warn groups they will have to work quickly to put their skits together. It will in fact boost the energy of small groups to have a bit of time pressure. If you are short of time, use Option B instead of C.	**Component 5** *Visions and Hopes for* *Women in the Church* pages 151–152
5 min.	**Closing Worship** Use "Shower of Blessings."	*Resources for Worship* page 176

Session 5
(Reading before the session: Stories IV and Chapter 11)

pages 108–113

10 min.

Opening Worship
Use "Litany for Naomi's Daughters."

Resources for Worship
pages 172–173

35 min.

Celebrating Our Common Work
Use Option C, Thinking about Our Successes.
If you think you may have additional time, use
Option A or B, Church Tour, as well.

Component 6
Celebrating Our Common Work
page 154,
pages 153–154

70 min.

New Creations
This evening is a time of creativity. Follow the
outline. Explain the options available, divide into
groups, and encourage the women to have fun
creating something new. Explain that next week
there will be time for groups to share what they have
created with one another.

Component 7
New Creations
pages 155–156

5 min.

Closing Worship
Use "Commissioning of the Spirit."

*Resources for Worship
and Ritual*
page 176

Session 6
(Reading before the session: Stories V and Chapter 12)

pages 114–117

5 min.

Opening Worship
Use "Invocation of the Spirit" or a worship ritual
created by the group in the last session.

*Resources for Worship
and Ritual*
page 171

20 min.

Give groups a time to share with one another what
they created in the previous session

40 min.

Moving On: Planning for the Future
Use the process described.

Component 8
Moving On
page 157

40 min.

Moving On: Naming Learning and Evaluation
Use the activities described.

page 157

15 min.

Closing Worship
Use "Receiving the Blessing of Generations of
Women" or a worship ritual created by the group in
the last session.

*Resources for Worship
and Ritual*
page 172

Option 5

A Book-Study Outline

The following discussion or reflection questions may be used to help groups or individuals reflect on what they read in each chapter.

hood? How do you think these events or circumstances shaped your own framework or that of your generation?

Welcome and Gathering

Option A

A. Introduction

The purpose of this part of the workshop is to gather the group, introduce the workshop and participants, and set the tone for the task ahead.

You may need:

name tags and markers, agenda outline on newsprint, newsprint or whiteboard and markers

Welcome the group. Provide name tags if needed. Have group members introduce one another by name. If group members are from different congregations or do not know one another, have participants say where they are from. Put up a draft agenda for the time together.

Briefly introduce the workshop. You may wish to provide some or all of the following information.

- history of the Naomi's Daughter's project, through which this workshop was developed (see the Introduction to this book, page 3)
- thanks to anyone who helped with preparation, introduce the leadership team
- review of the process (length of workshop, summary of agenda)
- notes on logistics (breaks, food, washrooms, etc.)

Option B

B. Introducing Ourselves

Gather in groups of three to five people. Ask each person to share briefly with the others in her group what it was that encouraged her to come to this workshop and what she had to leave behind in order to be here.

Gather back in the whole group and invite the group to share some of their hopes for this time together. Ask a recorder to note the key points on newsprint or whiteboard.

Option C	## C. Hat Creations

Option C

You will need:

C. Hat Creations

scissors, masking tape, coloured markers, glue sticks, old newspapers, transparent tape, and a variety of "hat decorating" items such as feathers, fake fur, ribbon, pictures cut from magazines, construction paper, tissue paper, etc.

Ask everyone to make herself a hat that says something about her and her generation. Ask the participants to be creative with the supplies you have provided. A simple hat base, suitable for decorating, can be made by folding a piece of newspaper into a 6" wide roll and taping it into a headband, which can then be embellished. More fancy hat designs are up to the participant's own creative imagination.

Encourage women, even those who don't think of themselves as "arty" types to experiment and have fun with the materials. Explain that they will have about 20 minutes to make a hat.

When the creations are finished, have people wear their creations. If you have time, have each woman say one or two words about her hat by asking, what does your hat say about you and about your generation?

Option D

You will need:

D. Making a Name for Ourselves

scissors, masking tape, glue sticks, coloured markers, construction paper, pictures cut from magazines, coloured tissue paper, pins

Ask everyone to make herself a nametag that says something about her and her generation. Ask the women to be creative with the supplies you have provided.

Encourage women, even those who don't think of themselves as "arty" types to experiment with shapes and colours. Explain that they will have about 15 minutes to make a nametag.

When the creations are finished, have people wear their nametags. Ask everyone to say one or two words about the nametag by asking: what does it say about you and about your generation?

Bible Study

Reflecting on the Story of Ruth and Naomi

You will need:

Bibles, pens and paper, flipchart or whiteboard and marker

This part of the workshop focuses on the biblical story of Ruth and Naomi, from the Book of Ruth, as a story about women relating across cultures and generations.

a. Introducing the Biblical Story

Gather in a circle. Explain that the story of Naomi and Ruth is an ancient story about a relationship between women of different generations. Invite participants to listen to the story and to notice what comes to mind for them as they think about relationships between women of different generations in the this story and in their own lives.

b. Hearing the Story of Ruth and Naomi

Shorter Option: Ask someone to read aloud Ruth 1:1–17. Ask those who know the whole story to fill in the details of what happcned in the saga of these women. Add details from your own knowledge of the story.

Longer Option: Invite someone who is skilled at telling stories to prepare to tell the story of Ruth or give people time to read all four chapters from the Bible for themselves.

c. Reflecting on the Story

Ask participants to pair up and discuss the following questions with the person sitting beside her:

1. What do you notice about the relationship between these women?
2. How do you feel about their relationship?

Gather back in the whole group. Ask:

1. What were some of the qualities in the relationship between Naomi and Ruth? Ask someone to record key words on newsprint—e.g. loyalty, courage.

2. What do you think this story has to say to us, in our lives today?

d. Background to the Story   pages 9–10

Present a summary of key information from the section entitled "Background to the Story of Ruth and Naomi," Chapter 1. If people have copies of the book, they might be asked to read this part of Chapter 1 for themselves.

Discuss: How did this information change or add to what you heard in the story of Ruth and Naomi?

Longer Option: **Relationships across Generations**
Invite people to form groups of four to six people. Ask them to think about a relationship that they have had with a woman of a different generation. It may have been a long time ago or more recent, a family member or not. Give groups enough time for each person to share her story and talk about how this relationship was different from or similar to the relationship between Ruth and Naomi.

e. Learning from the Story

Gather back in the whole group. Ask:

1. What do you think can be learned from this story about relationships between women across generations?

2. What vision does this story give you about relationships between women of different generations in the church?

3. What is your vision or hope for how women in our church could relate across generations?

Ask a recorder to record visions and hopes on newsprint.

f. Considering the Visions pages 10–12

Present a summary of key information in the section "Daughters of Naomi" from Chapter 1. If people have copies of the book, they might read this part of Chapter 1 for themselves.

In the whole group, discuss what other elements or ideas you would add to your hopes or visions for how women in our church could relate across generations, based on information from this chapter.

g. Final Thoughts

Take a few minutes to have people share in the circle any other insights, last thoughts, or questions they have about this story.

Storytelling with Timeline

Sharing Generation-Shaping Experiences and Stories of Women's Lives

This part of the workshop introduces the concept of generational frameworks and helps participants to hear the stories and events that shaped different generations of women.

A Note on the Timeline

The timeline helps women to recall and reflect in small age-specific groups, as they prepare to share the story of their generation.

As I reviewed this workshop design with others, I encountered a certain hesitation about using the timeline. Would it work for groups of women in more rural situations, for example, or women from areas that may not have been at the centre of some of the key events on the timeline? Would women even know about some of these events? Could they relate?

I had similar questions as I tested this. What I discovered is that the events on the timeline are meaningful for Canadian women in a variety of different settings, including rural ones, and across a range of cultures. This does not mean that all events on the timeline are meaningful for all women, of course.

The events on the timeline are intended to serve as a trigger and memory cue to help members of each generation recall what was going on in their time and context. This is by no means a comprehensive listing, nor even an attempt to say which events are most important. Women may add other events to the timeline and may find some events more significant than others. Gathering around the timeline also serves an important function for others in the group—a visual cue as to what was going on in the world at the time each generation reached adulthood.

You will need: *file cards in 4 or 5 colours, paper and pens, copies of "Introduction to Frameworks" (Handout 1, pages 158–159) and "Task for Small Groups" (Handout 2, page 160) for everyone, a timeline. To make the timeline, photocopy the timeline events (Handout 4, page 162–167) and paste them onto file cards in order of date. Use a long strip of yarn taped around the walls of the meeting area. Peg the file cards onto this yarn timeline using paper clips or masking tape to attach the cards. Space the cards well apart on the timeline.*

a. Introduction

Explain that the purpose of this part of the workshop is to hear stories and experiences from women of various age groups to better understand the differences and commonalities between women of different generations.

The story of Ruth and Naomi points us to a vision and possibility of relationships that span barriers of age, culture, and other differences. However, often in the church, we may find ourselves face to face with these blocks and barriers. The timeline exercise is a way to help each age group tell the stories and experiences that have shaped them. Hearing one another's stories and exploring the different world view and perspectives of different age groups is key to building common understanding and insight.

pages 158–159 Hand out copies of the article "Introduction to Frameworks," (Handout 1). Explain that this introduces this part of the workshop. Ask people to read it for themselves.

pages 33–47 *Alternative:* if group members are reading the book, invite them to read chapters 4 and 5 before the timeline activity.

b. Task for Small Groups

Divide into four age groups of roughly equal sizes: Group 1 (born before 1931); Group 2 (born 1932 to 1944); Group 3 (born 1945 to 1954); Group 4 (born after 1954). If you have a lot of younger women, create a fifth group: Group 5: (born after 1975).

Give each group file cards—at least one per person (use a different coloured card for each group), paper clips, and markers, notepaper and pen, and the Task for Small Groups (Handout 2, page 160). If you have a Group 5, give them Handout 3, page 161. Explain that groups will have about 15–20 minutes to talk together and complete their task. Remind each group to find a reporter for their conversation.

Ask groups to gather at the timeline roughly at the point on the timeline when most of their group was between the ages of thirteen to twenty-two. Groups may wish to pull some chairs to-gether as they gather at the timelines, to make it easier for them to see and hear each other. Ask them to notice the major events and changes in society that are on the timeline. Which events do they think were relevant and important to them at the time? Ask them to add other major events by writing the events on blank file cards.

Ask groups to write the names of women in their small group on file cards and peg them on the timeline at the approximate point where they turned fifteen. Explain that each group except the youngest (Group five) will think about this question: What key historical and social events occurred during the time when you were aged thirteen to twenty-two that shaped the lives of women in your generation? Note that this is not a question about per-sonal circumstances or local events, but major world-changing events, changes, or trends. Some examples are war, economic boon times, and so on, that affected most of the people in your generation, in your formative years. Events could be national or international (economic depression, war) or more regional (clos-ing of a mines or fishery, rural to urban migration, etc.). Ask each group to discuss: What has been the overall impact of these events or changes in society upon women of your generation? How do you think your generation was shaped or influenced by these events? Ask for a recorder to take notes and to prepare to report back on behalf of each group.

If you have a "group five" of youngest women, it will be very hard for them to identify how their generation is shaped by the events that are still forming this generation. Ask them instead to discuss and prepare to report back on the following questions: What do you think is happening in society/the world right now that is different for your generation than for previous ones? What would you like older generations of women to understand about your life right now? A different set of small group discus-sion questions is provided for this youngest age group, Task for Group Five, Handout 3, page 161.

c. Hear Generational Stories
Invite the whole group to gather at the point on the timeline where the oldest group of women has been meeting (the point where this group was roughly aged thirteen to twenty-one). Set out chairs for those who wish to sit. Others can stand, so that

everyone can see the timeline. Invite the whole group to notice what is on the timeline. Ask the first (oldest) group to report back briefly on their conversation, sharing some of the key events, and how these events may have shaped their generation's framework. The person with notes will start this; ask others in the group for events they would like to add. Continue through the next oldest group and so on to the youngest group of women, moving up the timeline. Keep careful track of time. Depending on the time you have available and the number of groups, you may have to limit the reporting time of each group (in shorter workshops you will have about 8 minutes per group for 5 groups, 10 minutes each for 4 groups; in longer workshops you may have up to 15 to 17 minutes per group).

d. Reflect on Generation-shaping Experiences
Gather in the whole group to discuss the following questions.
1. How are generations of women different because of these formative events or experiences?
2. How might these differences block communication or understanding between women of different generations?
3. What are some of the things that women have in common, across generations?

e. Discussion in Mixed-age Groups
Form four small groups of mixed ages to discuss the following questions.
1. How are generations of women different because of these formative events or experiences?
2. How might these differences block communication or understanding between women of different generations?
3. What are some of the things that women have in common, across generations?

Gather back together in the whole group for the question that follows.

What new insights did you gain from the storytelling at the timeline about the experiences of different generations and how generations were shaped by these experiences? Ask a recorder to take note of the key points, on newsprint or whiteboard.

Generations of Women in the Church

The goal of this activity is to discuss how generational differences between women have an impact on or affect how women participate in the church.

You will do either Option A or B. Option B is a short discussion option, Option A is a longer activity.

Option A

A. Fishbowl

Move into a "fishbowl" format (a circle of chairs in the middle, others around the outside as observers). Beginning with the youngest age group, ask that group to move into the fishbowl. Explain that this group will talk as the others listen without intervening. There will be a chance later for other groups to enter the fishbowl.

The facilitator moves into the fishbowl and invites the group in the fishbowl to discuss while others outside listen. Explain that the goal is for them to talk about their participation in the church and the issues that affect their generation's participation in the church. Use some of the following questions to get the conversation started, but don't interrupt the flow once the conversation gets going. Ask for a recorder outside the fishbowl to take detailed notes.

Questions to stimulate conversation:
1. What kind of priority do you give to participation in church?
2. Is church an optional activity for you, one choice among many, as more of a duty or obligation?
3. Do most women of your age group attend and participate in church life?
4. How central has the church been to the social and community life of women in your generation?
5. How do you think women of all ages should participate in the life of the church?

6. What do you value most about your church involvement?
7. How much authority does the church have in your life?

Repeat for the next youngest age group, through to the oldest, allowing about 5–7 minutes per group.

Gather back in the whole group. Discuss the following questions:
1. What new insights or ideas did you gain from listening to the fishbowl discussions?
2. As you think about the generational differences we have been discussing, how do you think these differences affect women's participation in the church?
3. What main issues or differences do you feel block women of different generations from coming together effectively in the church?
4. What do we have in common that helps us work together?

Option B

B. Group Discussion
Post the following questions on newsprint so that everyone can see them. Ask people to write their response to the following questions silently or to talk with the person beside them.
1. As you think about the generational differences we have been discussing, how do you think these differences affect women's participation in the church?
2. What main issues or differences do you feel block women of different generations from coming together effectively in the church?
3. What do we have in common that helps us work together?

Gather back in the whole group and discuss the responses to these questions.

Visions and Hopes for Women in the Church

You will need:

newsprint or whiteboard and markers; if you do the mural you will also need coloured markers and a large sheet of mural paper taped to wall.

Option A

A. Create Skits

Divide into four equal-sized groups of mixed ages.

Ask each group to create a short skit that depicts how you would like women of the United Church to be able to relate and work together across generations (i.e. depict in a skit what this might look like if women in the United Church really got along across age groups as you'd hoped or imagined we could). Gather back in the whole group and ask each small group to present its skit.

After each skit, ask each group to comment on some of the elements of their vision. Ask a recorder to record key ideas on newsprint. What are some of the common elements of the vision?

Option B

B. Naming Our Vision

Ask people to write their response to the following question silently: What is your vision or hope for how women in the United Church could relate across generations? Give as many concrete examples as you can.

Gather back in the whole group and invite the women to share their ideas.

Discuss what blocks us from achieving this vision? What can we do to make this vision a reality? Ask a recorder to note key points of the discussion on newsprint or whiteboard.

Option C

C. Vision Murals

Put up the mural paper, and invite the group to gather around it. Draw a vertical line down the middle of the mural paper. Ask everyone to work together to create a visual or verbal image of the kind of way you would hope women in the church could work together. They might draw or use a combination of images and words to describe the vision.

Use the right-hand side of the mural paper to create this description of the vision.

On the left-hand side of the mural paper have group members write things that block us from achieving this vision. Underline each block with an arrow pointing to the left (away from the vision). Use the length of the arrow to indicate how strong you think the block is—a short arrow would be a relatively minor block. Longer arrows would indicate bigger blocks. Still working on the left-hand side of the mural, write things that you think might help us achieve this vision. Use arrows or a different colour, pointing left to right (towards the vision) to indicate how strong or powerful you think each item in the "helps" list might be in getting us to the vision.

When the mural is complete, look at it together.

What do you notice? What do you wonder about? What can help us achieve our vision as women in the church?

Things that block us from

← achieving our vision

Things that block us from

← achieving our vision

Things that help us to

achieve our vision →

Visual drawing and

written description

of our vision here

Celebrating
Our Common Work

Option A

A. Church Tour

If you are taking a vitual tour, you will need symbols for each area (see below). Otherwise, you will need full access to the church building.

Take a tour of the church building, including rooms such as the kitchen, parlour, meeting or Sunday school rooms, sanctuary, and church office. As you gather in each area of the building ask:

1. What good things have women done here together? (Encourage the group to share stories and memories of that space.)
2. What would we like to do together in this place?

End with the church steps, to symbolize the mission of the church beyond the walls of the building itself, and phrase the question differently "what good things have women done together to be the church in action in the world? What would we like to do together to make a difference in the world?"

Option B

B. Virtual Tour

If you are not meeting in a church building, if all of your group are not from the same congregation, or if you have less time, go on a "Virtual Tour." Visit each imaginary room by visiting each of the stations in turn. Set up parts of the meeting area to represent rooms or spaces in a typical church building, and use the following symbols to designate each area:

1. Kitchen: A basin, kettle, and tea towel
2. Sanctuary: a hymnbook and candle stand
3. Meeting room: a flipchart stand or chair and table
4. Sunday school or Bible study room: a curriculum resource
5. Parlour: a fancy teacup or lamp
6. Church office: a telephone
7. Church steps: a coat and boots

As you gather in each area of the building ask:

1. What good things have women done here together? (Encourage the group to share stories and memories of that space.)
2. What would we like to do together in this place?

End with the church steps, to symbolize the mission of the church beyond the walls of the building itself, and phrase the question differently "what good things have women done together to be the church in action in the world? What would we like to do together to make a difference in the world?"

Option C	## C. Thinking about Our Successes
You will need:	*pens, paper, drawing pencils.*

Hand out paper, pens, and drawing pencils. Ask people to think about the following question: What are some of the success stories of women working well in your church (either together or in different age groupings)? Note that sometimes events or activities that take place separately, where there is mutual respect and cooperation, such as several different women's groups in one congregation, can also count as successes. Invite women to write, draw, or doodle as they think about this question.

Ask people to share their examples of successes and give details. Why do these count as successes? Does everyone think this story is a success? Note that some of us may have different reflections on the same experience—encourage honest, but gentle and respectful sharing of different opinions.

Discuss the following questions:

1. What do you think has helped make these successes possible?
2. What would you like to be doing with other women, across generations?

Based on what you have discovered during the workshop, are there things we need to take account of in our ongoing involvements and activities?

Have a recorder take notes or record main ideas on newsprint, as you may want to save these ideas for later planning.

New Creations

Present a variety of options for creative expression, based on what women have learned and experienced so far. Invite them to choose an area of creative expression, and find others who will work with them on the task. Not all options need to be covered. Write the description of each option on a file card and place it with the supplies needed in an area of the meeting room (or separate rooms if you have space). Explain each option and have women choose where they would like to go.

Option A

A. Creating Worship and Liturgy

You will need:

candles and matches; some objects that could be used in worship such as flowers, basin, jug, bread, etc.; a Bible and song books; writing paper and pens.

Create a simple worship experience, prayer, or ritual that would be appropriate for women across generations who are coming together to build trust, understanding, and communication. Really work together and don't compromise too easily—the resources you generate will then be ones that they are all truly comfortable with.

You might, for example, write a prayer or litany, prepare a meditation or drama or retelling of scripture, create a ritual (something that can be *done*, that involves movement and action—lighting of candles, pouring water, symbols), create a movement or dance, write a song. Use your imagination and creativity. Gather the resources you need for your ritual.

| **Option B** | **B. Planning an Event** |

You will need: *note paper and pens.*

Plan an ideal event for women across generations.
Include notes on
- where the event would take place
- who would go
- what would happen there
- why this event is important
- what *wouldn't* happen there etc.…

| **Option C** | **C. A Creative Expression through Visual Arts** |

You will need: *clay or modelling compound; paints, brushes, drawing paper, and pencils; arts and craft supplies such as construction paper, glue, scissors, tissue paper, markers, magazines that can be cut up.*

Create something that expresses what you have learned
or discovered in this event so far, how you are feeling
right now, at this point in the process, or something
that expresses your hope or vision for women in the
church. Use the art supplies creatively and have fun—
there is no right end product.

Moving On:

Next Steps, Evaluation, and Closing

Option A

A. Planning for the Future

Create a plan of action for women in your congregation working together across generations. Have a recorder take detailed notes of your plans. Ask yourselves the following questions:

1. What do we want to do or do differently? (our goal)
2. What obstacles might we need to address to achieve our goal?
3. Who might help or join with us?
4. What would we need to do to achieve this goal? (next steps)
5. Who will do what? (tasks and follow-up)

Option B

B. Naming Learning

Ask each person to think of one thing that they gained or learned from this workshop experience. Give people a few minutes to think about this before responding.

Alternatively, write the phrase "Because of this event I…" on newsprint and ask each person in turn to complete the sentence.

Option C

C. Evaluation

Ask everyone to complete and hand in an evaluation form (Handout 5, page 168). If you have time, ask each person to share a highlight of the experience and something they would recommend be done differently another time.

Introduction to Frameworks

Social scientists tell us that there are distinct differences between members of generations based on the context that shaped us during crucial formative years, the years in which each generation reaches adulthood. The critical years are roughly ages thirteen to twenty-two.

The historical and social events that occur, and the context in which people move into the adult world, shape each generation's culture and outlook on the world. Some use the term "framework" to describe this world view. Each generation has its own distinct framework.

Obviously the personal events that take place are also important, but this theory addresses what is going on in the wider world and how that shapes a whole generation's outlook. For example, the generation that spent its formative years during the depression or the Second World War was shaped or influenced differently from the generation that spent its formative years in the boom times of the 1950s or the social upheaval and crisis years of the 1960s and 1970s.

For someone shaped by the 1960s and 1970s—a time of immense social upheaval and change—change may be seen as normal and to be expected. Members of that generation will not only expect that change does and will occur (because it has always been part of their world) but will also expect that they can to some degree control and influence change. For someone whose formative years were the Second World War years, change may be viewed not as normal but as an aberration. In their life experience, the world was soon going to return to "the way things were"—for them, change might be anything but "normal."

Someone socialized in a period of affluence and stability may view the use of resources very differently from someone raised during scarcity, war, or economic reces-sion. Someone socialized in an era of cutbacks, unemployment, and downsizing may view the future very differently from someone who grew up in a time of economic growth.

Although these generational "frameworks," or ways of looking at the world, obviously do not define all of who we are, they can sometimes block understanding and communication across generations. The more we can understand about our own framework, and that of others, the better we will be able to appreciate and understand the differences between us.

A generational framework is a description of a mindset or way of apprehending the world. It is not a description of values or beliefs. For example, people who come from a generation for which change is both positive and normal (for example, someone whose formative years took place in the late 1960s and early 1970s) might tend to seem themselves as agents of change. Their perspective might be: I/we have the power to make changes; I/we can change this for the better, etc. However, this says nothing about the values or direction of change—change might be very "me" focused or altruistic, it might be directed towards technological "progress" or world peace, getting ahead in the world or ending injustice.

People might challenge the notion of frameworks by noting that "I know women in their eighties who are strong feminists, and women in their thirties who are opposed to feminism." But the theory of frameworks doesn't say anything about these kinds of values—of course there have been people who have worked for justice for women for many decades (for example, those who fought for temperance or for the vote for women). A framework is more of a cultural approach than it is a set of values or beliefs.

A generational framework, once it exists, is also available to all previous generations. Once it exists as a framework, others from previous generations may and can adopt it. It would be an extreme over-generalization to say that all people of a given generation hold on to their generation's framework for a lifetime. Most do, of course, but many don't. Most within a generation raised in the Depression and war years may view change as bad and not normal (we'll soon get back to the way things were). But some within their own generation may have adopted the framework of subsequent generations (the optimism of the 1950s generation, for example, or the more proactive, change-initiating framework of the 1960s crowd).

Understanding more about the particular framework of our own generation can help us understand more about ourselves and how we view the world differently from other generations. We might ask ourselves, what was going on in our world during the years when we were thirteen to twenty-two, and how was our generation shaped or influenced by that? We can also gain perspective on other generations by hearing how they address these same questions.

Task for Small Groups

Storytelling with Timeline

Make sure someone in your group takes notes and is prepared to report back on behalf of your group.

Gather at the timeline roughly at the point on the timeline when most members of your group were between the ages of thirteen to twenty-two. You may wish to pull some chairs together, to make it easier to see and hear each other, or you may be comfortable standing.

Write your own names on file cards and peg them on the timeline at the approximate point where you turned fifteen. Notice the major events and changes in society that are on the timeline (these are triggers only to jog your memory about those years). Think of other major events that shaped your generation during these formative years. Write the events on blank file cards.

Discuss the following questions:

1. What key historical and social events occurred during the time when you were aged thirteen to twenty-two that shaped the lives of women in your generation? Note: this is not a question about personal circumstances or local events, but major world-changing events, changes, or trends. For example, war, economic boon times, etc., that affected most of the people in your generation, in your formative years. Events could be national or international in scope (economic depression, war) or more regional (closing of the fishery, rural to urban migration, etc.)

2. What has been the overall impact of these events or changes in society upon women of your generation? In other words, how do you think your generation was shaped or influenced by these events or changes?

Task for Group Five *(women born after 1975)*

Storytelling with Timeline

Make sure someone in your group takes notes and is prepared to report back on behalf of your group.

Gather at the point on the timeline where the oldest members of your group turned thirteen. Write your name on a file card and add it to the timeline at the point where you turned fifteen, or, if you are not yet fifteen, at this current year. Notice the events on the timeline, from 1988 onwards. Which other events would you add that are significant to your generation? Write these events on file cards and add them to the timeline.

Discuss the following questions:
1. What do you think is happening in society/the world right now that is different for your generation than for previous ones?
2. What are the main event/trends/issues in society right now that affect your generation?
3. What would you like older generations of women to be able to under-stand about your life and what it is like for you as you enter adulthood?

Creating a Timeline

Cut the dates apart and tape them to file cards, or photocopy the date sheets onto #08162 4"x 1 1/3" labels and stick them to file cards (one date per card). Attach file cards, in order, to a long piece of yarn that has been taped around the meeting room. For some years, there is more than one card. Use paper clips or masking tape to hang the dates on the timeline. Space dates well apart—you may have to go around several walls of the room.

1929 Wall Street stock exchange crashes	1935 drought, vast dust storms in US and Canadian prairies
1930 unemployment soars throughout industrialized world, Cairine Wilson becomes Canada's first female senator	1936 Spanish Civil War begins, Germany defies Versailles Treaty
1933 Hitler appointed Chancellor of Germany	1937 Japanese attack Beijing
1934 100,000 Chinese communists led by Mao Zedong, begin the Long March	1938 Germany annexes Austria

1938   Kristallnacht (the Night of Broken Glass) when hundreds of synagogues and Jewish businesses were destroyed throughout Germany and Austria

1939   Germany invades Poland; Second World War begins; France, Britain declare war; Canada and rest of Commonwealth join them

1940   Auschwitz constructed; Germany captures Norway, Holland, Belgium, Denmark, half of France

1940   women get right to vote in Québec (last province to give women vote)

1941   Japan bombs US fleet at Pearl Harbor

1942   US and Canada round up citizens of Japanese origin to be held in camps

1943   Jews of Warsaw Ghetto massacred

1945   Allied troops capture Berlin, US drops atomic bombs on Hiroshima and Nagasaki, end of Second World War, Hitler dead, Auschwitz "discovered"

1946   First UN General Assembly meets

1947   India and Pakistan win independence from Britain, US President Truman calls for crusade against communists

1948   Gandhi assassinated, Palestinian civil war erupts, first Arab-Israeli war

1949   Mao proclaims People's Republic of China, USSR explodes first nuclear bomb, NATO formed, Germany partitioned

1950   North Korea invades the South, Jordan annexes the West Bank

1951   South Africa removes vote from people of mixed race

1952 South African National Congress campaigns against racist laws	**1960** Sharpville massacre in South Africa—police open fire on unarmed crowd
1953 Armistice signed, ending Korean war	**1961** number of military US "advisers" in Vietnam reaches 16,000
1954 US rules racially segregated schools illegal	**1962** Cuban missile crisis
1955 Nikita Khruschev takes power in USSR, Warsaw Pact formed (Cold War heats up), Rosa Parks makes history with refusal to give up seat reserved for whites	**1963** Martin Luther King Jr. gives "I have a dream…" speech, President J. F. Kennedy assassinated
1956 Britain and France seize Panama Canal, contraceptive pill is produced, Russian invasion of Hungary	**1964** Palestine Liberation Organization formed, Nelson Mandela given life imprisonment
1957 1,000 US federal troopers enforce desgregation in Little Rock, Arkansas	**1964** civil rights movement, race riots in US, Vietnam war escaltes, Ontario rules racially segregated schools illegal
1959 Fidel Castro's rebels take power in Cuba	**1965** US planes bomb North Vietnam

1966 race riots erupt in US cities, Mao launches cultural revolution	**1971** Greenpeace, and North American environmental movement are born, civil war in Pakistan results in famine in Bangladesh
1967 China explodes first H-bomb, US uses bombs, napalm in Vietnam	**1972** Idi Amin expels 50,000 Asians from Uganda, US escalates Vietnam bombing
1967 Canadian centennial, De Gaulle visits Montreal and says "Vive le Québec libre"	**1973** Paris Peace Accord signed ending US involvement in Vietman, Arab oil producers increase oil prices by 70%
1968 Martin Luther King assassinated	**1973** US-backed coup in Chile overthrows elected President Allende
1969 moon walk, British troops deployed in Northern Ireland,	**1974** Watergate scandal, President Nixon resigns
1969 riots at Sir George Williams University, Montréal, around issue of racism	**1974** in Uganda Idi Amin conducts ruthless purge (250,000 already killed under his regime)
1970 FLQ kidnaps and murders Pierre Laport, Trudeau invokes emergency powers	**1975** United Nations declares International Women's Year

1976	school children in Soweto township, South Africa, lead protest against apartheid, Parti Québecoise elected

1976-1985	UN Declares Decade for Women

1977	refugees flee Communist rule in Vietnam (over 110,000 refugees by end of 1990), Vietnamese boat people come to Canada,

1977	South African rights leader Stephen Biko killed in police custody

1978	First UN Special Session on Disarmament; Prime Minister Pierre Trudeau reaffirms Canada's commitment not to build, test, use, or store nuclear weapons

1979	Margaret Thatcher elected PM in Britain

1980	El Salvador's Archbishop Oscar Romero shot by paramilitaries

1980	Québec votes against independence

1981	Ronald Reagan elected US President

1981	El Salvador civil war begins (refugees flee), oil prices triple

1982	Bertha Wilson becomes first women judge appointed to Canadian Supreme Court

1983	Ronald Reagan reveals Star Wars defence plan, massive protests in Europe against controversial Cruise missiles

1985	movement for sanctions against South Africa grows worldwide

1986	USSR nuclear reactor in Chernobyl explodes, nuclear pollution spreads over most of Europe

1989	Chinese students occupy Tiananmen Square, Berlin Wall torn down, Communist rule ends in Czechoslovakia
1989	80 nations sign treaty to end use of CFCs, US and USSR sign first treaty to cut nuclear weapons
1989	Mohawks occupy ancestral land near Oka, Québec, leading to armed standoff
1990	Nelson Mandela released from prison, Germany reunited, USSR disintegrates
1991	Operation Desert Storm in Kuwait
1991	South African apartheid legally ended
1991	war breaks out in Yugoslavia

1992	referendum narrowly rejects Québec independence
1992	civil war ends in El Salvador
1992	Earth Summit in Rio makes small progress on environmental issues
1993	US troops clash with thousands of protesters in Mogadishu, Somalia
1994	Rwanda Hutus massacre almost a million Tutsis
1995	Fourth UN Conference on women in Beijing
1997	Ottawa Treaty banning anti-personnel landmines is signed

Workshop Evaluation Form

What new insights or learning did you gain from this workshop about different generations of women within the church?

_____

_____

_____

_____

_____

_____

Which activities in the workshop do you think were the best for your own learning? Why?

_____

_____

_____

_____

_____

_____

Which activities in the workshop do you think were the best for building communication between women across generations? Why?

_____

_____

_____

_____

_____

_____

What changes would you recommend for future workshops?

_____

_____

_____

_____

_____

Other comments:

_____

_____

_____

_____

_____

Resources for Worship and Ritual

These worship and liturgical resources are designed to be self-contained. Although there were designed and tested for this particular book and workshop process, they can be adapted for use at different events or in other settings. They are intended primarily for small-group use, with women of different generations who have gathered together.

They also may be combined into a longer time of worship or meditation. To create a simple worship outline, choose an item from each of the three categories:

A. Openings and Invocations,

B. Rituals for Generations of Women, and

C. Closing Prayers and Blessings.

Add a couple of music selections from D, such as a hymn of praise or invocation to open, and a hymn of sending forth.

It is permitted to copy any of these prayers for use in small group worship. Please do not distribute copies for other purposes.

A. Openings and Invocations

God of All the Ages

Set two candles in holders on the worship table. The leader will invite the oldest and youngest women in the group to each light a candle (the group may need to confer briefly to figure out who among them is the oldest and youngest.)

Prayer (in unison)
God of all the ages,
God of the young, the old, and the in-between
God of women, men, and children,
God of each one of us gathered here,
We gather in your name.
Open our eyes and ears and hearts to experience you in our midst.
Open our eyes and ears and hearts to hear your truth spoken and your love expressed in all that we do this day. Amen.

Ritual of Lines into Circles
You will need a candle in a holder and matches, a recording of quiet, meditative music and a tape or CD player.

You will need a large open space, with enough room for participants to form a line. If some participants have difficulty standing, arrange for a few chairs to be available. This ritual can be playful and relaxed in tone. Participants will need to talk as they form lines. Place a lit candle on a small table or stand in the centre of the space. Invite the group to form a line at one end of the room. Ask them to rearrange themselves by height; then again by birthplace (on a continuum from east to west); and finally by age.

When the group has created this final line, ask them to pause for a moment of silence to reflect on the lines they have created. Say the following prayer:

Prayer (in unison)
O God, when lines of age or experience divide us, draw us into a circle.
When lines of class, culture, race, or geography alienate us, draw us into a circle.
When lines get crossed, and miscommunication abounds, draw us into a circle.
The circle of your love is wide, O God. There is room for all our differences, there is room for all our experiences, there is room for all. Draw us into a circle, O God, that we may hear your voice and see your face.

The leader will put on the quiet music and invite the group to very slowly move the line into a circle, gathered around the lit candle. When the circle is complete, pause for a moment of silence. The leader will say "Amen" or "Blessed be."

Look into My Eyes
The leader will invite the group to gather in a circle, and look into one another's faces as the poem is read. Look deeply, as you open yourselves to one another and to the presence of God's Spirit.

Litany (for three voices)
Voice 1:
Look into my eyes
And see the wisdom of my years
The courage and the insight that I bring
The spark of holy light that dwells in me.
Look into my eyes, and see God's truth.
Voice 2:
Look into my face
And see the traces of the years
The smile of youth, the graceful curve of lines
Where laughter etched her passing.

See the lines that time has drawn, the map of pass-
ing days
Or journeys yet untravelled, roads yet to come.
Look into my face and see the marks upon this
holy page
That God has drawn.
Voice 3:
Look into my eyes, my sister, friend, companion on
the way,
And see that you and I are bearers of God's love.

Invocation of the Spirit

Say the meditation, using your own words. Speak slowly.
Pause to let the women breathe and reflect.

I invite you to pause for a moment and breathe
very deeply. The spirit of God, *ruach* [roo-ahk] in
Hebrew, *pneuma* [new-ma] in Greek, means wind
or breath. Think of the spirit of God as the life-
giving breath of God. Breathe in, and think of
drawing in the breath of God, deep into your being. (Pause) As you breathe, think of God's Holy
Spirit breathing in and around you. (Pause)

At the very beginning of creation, the Bible
tells us, the spirit of God was moving like a wind,
as God breathed over the waters of creation. Let
God's Spirit move over you, breathe over you,
breathe into you a sense of wholeness and life.
(Pause) Let the breath of God's Spirit enliven you,
let it connect you to yourself, to this place, to this
group. May the breath of God's Spirit move
around and over us, and over all that we do in this
time together. In our listening and in our speech,
in our thinking and in our doing, may we be God's
creation, breathed into being by God's holy breath.
Amen.

B. Rituals for Generations of Women

Receiving the Blessing of Generations of Women

If women in the group do not know one another well, this ritual would work best later in a workshop process, after participants have had a chance to meet one another, or as a closing. You will need a recording of joyful music and a CD or tape player.

Invite group members to pair up, choosing as a partner someone who is of a different age group than themselves. Encourage the group to create as wide an age span as possible for their groupings. If the group is uneven in number, the leader joins a pair. When everyone has found a partner, ask the pairs to share briefly their responses to the following questions:

- what gift or contribution do you think your age-group has to offer to other generations of women in the church?
- what gift or contribution do you receive from the age-group represented by the person you are paired with?

Give pairs 5 minutes for this conversation and then form two lines about 4 feet apart. Pairs will now be facing each other, with one partner on each side of the line. Have each woman share *in one or two words* a gift, offered or received, that was identified in the conversation. As each pair shares, they may raise their arms upward to form an arch. The hands should not touch at the top of the arch. When the arch is complete, put on the lively music, and explain that the arch created with our arms is a sign of blessing. It reminds us of the blessing of the gifts we receive from one another. Ask the pair at one end of the line to join hands and skip, run, dance, walk (as the Spirit moves

them) through the arch and reform their arch at the other end of the line. Continue until everyone has had a chance to symbolically "receive the blessing of many generations of women."

Litany for Naomi's Daughters

You will need small self-sticking notes (3-5 per woman) and pens. Before you begin the litany, ask women to write on each of the sticky notes (one name per note) the names of women from another generation who have been significant to them—women they have known or women from the past who have been important in their lives (names might include biblical women). Write the litany on a large sheet of paper and post it on the wall. Before the litany is read, ask women to post (literally, stick on the paper) the names of women they would like to have named at that part of the litany. Ask five readers to read the parts of the litany. The readers for that section read the names aloud at that point in the litany.

Litany

Reader one: Naomi has many daughters, women like Ruth who have chosen loyalty and commitment and care, who have chosen to love with respect, women like …. (other women are named)

Reader two: Naomi has many daughters, women like Ruth, who have risked and dared to step beyond borders and across boundaries, women like…. (other women are named)

Reader three: Naomi has many daughters, women who have befriended women outside their class, or age, or culture, or experience; women with wisdom to see beyond stereotypes; women who have known how to be a true companion, friend or mentor; women like …. (other women are named)

Reader four: Naomi has many daughters, women who dare to ask for justice, who have stood up for their own rights or defended the rights of others, women who are not afraid of what others might think, women who have carved new roads where none have gone before, women like …. (other women are named)

Reader five: Naomi has many daughters, women of faith who witness to the truth of God's enduring love, women who bear the image of God, women who live the hope of God, women like …. (other women are named)

Reader one: Naomi has many daughters, women like Ruth, women like you, women like me. So let us celebrate with joy all of Naomi's daughters!

Psalm of Thanksgiving

Psalm 105 joyfully proclaims God's faithfulness throughout many generations. The psalmist declares how God's covenant love is revealed though Abraham and Isaac, Jacob, Joseph, Moses… This psalm borrows some of the language from Psalm 105 to celebrate the ways God's love is revealed through many generations of women.

Psalm

(read in two parts, alternating verses)

Group one: Give thanks to God and praise God's name,
Make known to everyone
the wonderful things that God has done.

Group two: Sing praises, sing praises!
Tell of God's wonderful works.

Group one: When Hagar was sent out into the desert, she was left to die.
Yet God heard her cry,
and she became the mother of many nations.

Group two: In the time of harsh oppression,
when the people lived under the cruel whip of the Pharaoh,
God sent the midwives, Shiphrah and Puah
who by their courage

defied the mighty Pharaoh
and protected the children.

Group one: God gave Miriam a song and helped her to lead her people
in the great dance of liberation.

Group two: In the time of the judges,
Naomi was weak and of no account,
a woman in a harsh land,
a stranger fleeing famine and loss,

Group one: Yet, God did not abandon her
but showed her steadfast love.

Group two: Though Ruth's loyalty and courage,
Naomi was led from death to life.
God was with her, guiding and protecting.

Group one: When Hannah had all but given up hope,
disgraced and shunned in the eyes of her people,
God heard her cry
and showered her with blessings.

Group two: By your servants and prophets,
your people have been blessed.

Group one: Through the peacemaking of Abigail,
the wisdom of Deborah, and the courage of Esther,

Group two: Through the openness of Mary,
the friendship of Mary and Martha,
the ministry of Dorcas, the persistence of Lydia,
your people have been blessed
throughout all generations.

All: Praise God!

Litany of Women's Lives through the Ages

You will need: a central table with a cloth, a dish of soil and seeds, a loaf of bread, a few small twigs, a candle with holder and matches, a basin with water and a washcloth, construction paper, scissors and markers, flowers. Divide up parts. Depending on your group size, women may read more than one part.

At each point in the reading, suggestions are made for how these symbols may be used. Different women in the group will be invited to bring forward the symbols and read parts of the litany.

Voice one: God, we recall with deep gratitude the women who have gone before us, our mothers and grandmothers and great-grandmothers, our ancestors in faith, those who have led the way.

Voice two: Generation after generation women have tilled the soil and planted the seeds, bearers of life they have brought forth life, generation upon generation.

(Dish of soil is placed on the centre and seeds are sprinkled into the soil.) Generation upon generation women have tended life, and defended it.

Voice three: They have harvested the fruits of the earth, kneaded the bread, set the table, fed the hungry, nourished the soul.

(Loaf of bread is placed on the table.)

Voice four: Generation after generation, women have knelt at the hearthside to fan the flames. By their hands they have provided warmth of welcome, shelter from the storm, and warmth for the heart.

(Twigs are arranged in a small pile like setting kindling, a candle is placed nearby and lit.) Women have lit candles of hope, sparked change, illumined injustice.

Voice five: Women's hands, generation upon countless generation, have bathed babies, washed dishes, wiped fevered foreheads, washed clean and wiped dry.

(Water is poured into the basin, the cloth is dipped in, wrung out, and draped on the edge of the bowl.) Outpoured water has cleansed, and has transformed.

Voice six: Throughout the ages, women have prayed, preached, and prophesied. They have sung hymns and shouted out psalms of joy. Their faith has nurtured faith, their vision has inspired vision.

(Open Bible is placed upon the table.)

Construction paper and scissors are handed out to the group. Each woman is asked to cut a simple shape to symbolize some contribution of women throughout the ages that they would like to honour. Symbols are placed on the table.

Voice seven: We give thanks for the lives of women throughout the ages. We honour them, and give thanks for their lives. *(Flowers are placed on the table.)*

C. Closing Prayers and Blessings

Closing Prayer

God, we thank you for this time together, and for all that we have learned.

May we continue to grow in knowledge, understanding, love, and compassion, as we continue our journey as your faithful people. Amen.

Ritual of Thanks

Invite the group to stand (as they are able) in a circle. This simple movement prayer uses arm gestures to convey a prayer of thanksgiving. Introduce and demonstrate each movement first, and then slowly say the prayer as the group joins in the movements with you.

We give thanks for all the gifts we have received during this time together. (*hold hands cupped in front of you*)

We give thanks for the gifts from the earth that sustain us and nourish us—for the food we shared together, for this space, for this holy earth. (*move arms downward and slightly to the sides, palms open, to acknowledge and give thanks for the gifts of the earth*)

We give thanks for this community (*join hands in a circle*) and for each one of us here, for the gifts we have received from one another,

And for the presence of God's Spirit with us. (*still with hands joined, move arms upward and in towards the centre of the circle*)

As we leave this place, may we go ready and willing to share the gifts we have received. (*move hands out in front of you, palms up and flat, in a gesture of offering*)

Amen.

Closing Ritual with Ribbons

You will need: *a candle and matches, 1"-wide coloured ribbon cut into 8" long pieces (at least one per person and in many different colours and textures) and pens that will write on the ribbon (permanent markers, laundry markers, some ballpoint or fine-tipped markers will also work). Write the closing prayer on newsprint and post it where all can see it.*

Place a lighted candle and coloured ribbons on a low table in the centre of the circle. Ask everyone to take a pen and a coloured ribbon. Ask them to write on the ribbon something for which they give thanks, using a single word. It might be a word that jumps out at them from the conversation, or from the story of Ruth and Naomi; it could be a name, an idea, a commitment, or a hope. When everyone has written her word, ask them to place the ribbons back around the candle, weaving the ribbons together into a single twisted strand as they do so. Each participant might speak her word aloud as she adds her ribbon, if she wishes.

Prayer (in unison)

God of Naomi and Ruth, God of countless generations of women, God of each one of us gathered here, we thank you for this time. We thank you for the stories we have heard and shared, for the ways our own stories are woven and intertwined with your unfolding tale of love and care. Inspire our vision, renew our hope, and bind us close to one another and to you, now and always. Amen.

Shower of Blessings (read responsively)

One: May you be blessed with wisdom,
All: May you be blessed with truth,
One: May you be blessed with vision,
All: May you be blessed with hope,
One: May you be blessed in your youth,
All: Blessed in old age,
One: Blessed in your understanding,
All: And blessed with many questions.
One: May what you hear be blessed,
All: And blessed be all you say.
One: May God shower blessings upon you, beloved of God,
All: That we may love and be loved, as women who bear God's image.
Amen.

Commissioning of the Spirit

Go with joy, thankful for this gathering,
Go with vision, inspired by the hopes of countless generations of women,
Go with strength, renewed by God's powerful spirit,
Go in love, assured that you are beloved of God,
Go with courage, challenged by what you have seen and heard,
Go in peace, soothed by the gentle breath of God.
Amen

D. Hymn Suggestions from Voices United

Faith of our fathers, faith of our mothers #580 (commitment, past generations)
Now thank we all our God. #236 (praise and thanks)
God is the one #283 (invocation, joining together)
Spirit of the living God # 376 (invocation, opening prayer)
Spirit of gentleness # 375 (Holy Spirit, faith history)
Teach me God to wonder #299 (openness to one another)
Open my eyes #371 (opening to one another)
Come Now, O God of peace #34 (unity in God's Spirit)
Let there be light #679 (prayer for understanding)
Though ancient walls #691 (breaking down of divisions)
Blest be the tie that binds #602 (commitment to one another)
In loving partnership #603 (seeking loving community)

Appendix

Participant Worksheet
This worksheet was used in the Naomi's Daughters workshops that were held to develop this book.

Visions and Hopes
1. What is your vision or hope for how women in the United Church could relate across generations? Give examples.

_____

_____

_____

_____

_____

_____

_____

Generational Differences
2. What key historical and social events occurred during the time when you were aged thirteen to twenty-two that shaped the lives of women in your generation? (E.g. events such as war, economic boon, etc. that affected most of the people in your generation.)

_____

_____

_____

_____

_____

_____

_____

3. How do you think your generation of women was influenced or affected by these events?

_____

_____

_____

_____

_____

4. What would you like women of other generations to know about your life—i.e. things that would help them understand you better?

_____

_____

_____

_____

_____

_____

_____

_____

_____

5. How do you think the differences between women of different generations have an impact or effect upon the United Church?

_____

_____

_____

_____

_____

_____

_____

_____

6. What do you think are the main reasons that women of different generations in the United Church tend to work and meet in different age-groups? What differences or divisions (if any)

have you noticed between women of different age groups in the United Church?

_____

_____

_____

_____

_____

_____

_____

_____

Success Stories

7. What things do women of all generations have in common that help us work together in the church?

_____

_____

_____

_____

_____

_____

_____

8. What are some of the "success stories" of women working together well in your church (either together or in different age groupings)?

_____

_____

_____

_____

_____

_____

_____

9. What do you think has helped make these successes possible?

_____

_____

_____

_____

_____

_____

10. What would you most like to do with other women of other generations?

_____

_____

_____

_____

_____

_____

_____

_____

Resources and Tools

11. What resources, tools, or ideas might help us bridge generational differences, overcome blocks to working together, or contribute to more 'success stories'?

_____

_____

_____

_____

_____

_____

12. If you could imagine an ideal cross-generational event for women, what would it be like?

_____

_____

_____

_____

_____

_____

_____

Sources

Bibby, Reginald W. *Mosaic Madness: The Poverty and Potential of Life in Canada*. Toronto: Stoddart, 1990

———. *Social Trends Canadian Style*. Toronto: Stoddart, 1995

———. *Unitrends*. Toronto: Department of Stewardship Services of The United Church of Canada, 1994

———. *Unknown Gods: The Ongoing Story of Religion in Canada*. Toronto: Stoddart, 1993

Canadian Advisory Council on the Status of Women. *Women and Work*. Ottawa: Canadian Advisory Council on the Status of Women, 1978

The Canadian Encyclopedia, Edmonton: Hurtig Publishers, 1988

Evans, Patrick and Gerda Wekerle, eds. *Women and the Canadian Welfare State: Challenges and Change*. Toronto: University of Toronto Press, 1997

Foote, David. *Boom, Bust & Echo*. Toronto: MacFarlane Walter & Ross, 1996

Hall, Douglas. "Our New Challenge: Speak Hope from the Wilderness" *The United Church Observer*, January, 2000

McClung, Nellie. *In Times Like These* Toronto: University of Toronto Press, 1972

Mead, Margaret. *Culture and Commitment*. Garden City, New York: Doubleday, 1970

Muir, Elizabeth. Unpublished paper written for the Department of Steward Services, The United Church of Canada, 1998.

Phillips, Paul and Erin Phillips. *Women and Work: Inequality in the Canadian Labour Market*. Toronto: James Lorimer and Company, 1993

Walrath, Douglas Alan. *Frameworks: Patterns of Living and Believing Today*. New York: The Pilgrim Press, 1987

Year Book and Directory 1996. Toronto: United Church of Canada, 1996

For Further Reading

Reginald W. Bibby. *Mosaic Madness: the Poverty and Potential of Life in Canada*. Toronto: Stoddart, 1990

Bibby examines the "Canadian mosaic" looking at changing patterns in attitudes, behaviour, and relationships in society.

Reginald W. Bibby. *Unknown Gods: The Ongoing Story of Religion in Canada*. Toronto: Stoddart, 1993

An examination of changes in the religious practices and beliefs of Canadians, in patterns of belief and attendance, as well as changes in beliefs among those who are not active members of any organized religious group.

Reginald W. Bibby. *Social Trends Canadian Style*. Toronto: Stoddart, 1995

A very readable statistical overview of Canadian opinions, values, attitudes, lifestyles, and how these have changed over the last sixty to seventy years.

Patrick Evans and Gerda Wekerle, eds. *Women and the Canadian Welfare State: Challenges and Change*. Toronto: University of Toronto Press, 1997

A collection of essays on issues affecting women. Of particular interest is an essay by Meg Luxton and Ester Reiter on women's experiences of work and family in Canada between 1980 and 1995.

Sylvia Fraser, ed. *A Woman's Place: Seventy Years in the Lives of Canadian Women*. Toronto: Key Porter Books, 1997

A look at the changes in the lives of Canadian women from 1925 to the present, as seen through the eyes of *Chatelaine* magazine.

Nellie McClung. *In Times Like These* University of Toronto Press: Toronto, 1972

A wonderful collection of McClung wisdom that "tells it like it is."

Margaret Mead. *Culture and Commitment* Doubleday: Garden City, New York, 1970

An excellent, enlightening, and surprisingly contemporary analysis of the "generation gap" in the modern world.

Paul Phillips and Erin Phillips. *Women and Work: Inequality in the Canadian Labour Market*. Toronto: James Lorimer and Company, 1993

Jim Taylor, ed. *Fire and Grace: Stories of History and Vision*. Toronto: United Church Publishing House, 1999

This anthology of personal reflections, stories, and essays written by more than fifty people looks back at the United Church over the past seventy-five years of its history.

Douglas Alan Walrath. *Frameworks: Patterns of Living and Believing Today* New York: The Pilgrim Press, 1987

An insightful description of the generational "frameworks" or mindsets in our church today, and the implications for how different generations relate, communicate, and participate in the life of the church.

Douglas Alan Walrath. *Options: How to Develop and Share Christian Faith Today* New York: The Pilgrim Press, 1988

An examination of the implications of different generational frameworks on patterns of belief, and the implications for how we share our faith in the world.